HERITAGE

A STUDY OF THE DISRUPTION

BY

G. D. HENDERSON, D.D., D.Litt.

PROFESSOR OF CHURCH HISTORY
UNIVERSITY OF ABERDEEN

FOREWORD BY
The Very Rev. P. D. THOMSON, D.D.
CONVENER OF THE CENTENARY COMMITTEE
OF THE CHURCH OF SCOTLAND

OLIVER AND BOYD LTD.
EDINBURGH - - - TWEEDDALE COURT
LONDON · 98 GREAT RUSSELL STREET, W.C.
1943

CONTENTS

FOREWORD

AT the request of the General Assembly of the Church of Scotland this book was written by Professor G. D. Henderson, of the Chair of Church History in Aberdeen University, as part of the arrangements made in commemoration of the Disruption of 1843, and in thanksgiving for the union of the Churches in 1929. The Assembly are indebted to him for undertaking this somewhat difficult task, and for discharging it with fulness of historical knowledge, and with fairness to both sides in the great debate of 100 years ago. For his treatment of the subject, and for all statements made and views expressed in the book, Professor Henderson is alone responsible.

As its main title denotes, *Heritage* includes a wider field of interest than the Disruption itself, central and supremely significant though that event is to the plan of the book. It opens with the challenge confronting the Church in the world of our time, a challenge by no means unprecedented or even rare in its agelong and chequered history. Many hammers have been worn out on this anvil. It concludes with the preparedness of the Church of Scotland to meet this challenge, disciplined as it has been by the trials through which it has passed from pre-Reformation to Disruption days, and enriched during the years of separation by the witness and achievement of its several communions, now unified in a Church which embraces the main elements of Scottish Presbyterianism.

Within these brackets lies the main theme of the book, described in the sub-title as " A Study of the Disruption." The Disruption, however, epoch-making though the author declares it to be, is but an incident in a great movement. It is the crucial episode in a long and often bitter struggle with the State from Reformation times onwards. This movement reaches its culmination in the recognition by the State in its Acts of 1921 and 1925 of the Church's spiritual freedom, and received fulfilment in the union of 1929. It is also the crowning instance in Scotland of a tension within the Church as a whole, which has always been present and probably always will be, and which had found many previous expressions in Scottish Church history as in that of the Church at large. Moderate and Evangelical were differing but complementary Christian types. The quarrel of the Church as a whole was with the State, and the resulting disruption was from the State, but the tension within the Church itself became acute, and, true to their deepest Christian convictions, the parties at variance followed their separate ways.

All this and much more Professor Henderson sets forth in brief compass, with vividness and verve, intimate knowledge of the period, insight into the issues involved, freshness of contemporary evidence, and skill in presentation. Against a religious and social background as their setting he etches with swift, sure strokes the personalities, the scenes, the heightening tension, and the moving climax of a drama that thrilled the soul of Scotland as few occasions have done in all her stormy history ; and through it all he traces the hand of God guiding His Church and girding it to its contemporary task.

Heritage is *popular* in the best sense of the word, and is to be heartily commended not to ministers, office-bearers, and members of the Church alone, but to all who, open-eyed to present-day events, discern in the Gospel the ultimate fount and source of freedom, and in the Church when it is true to the Gospel the most powerful of all bulwarks against oppression. *Nec tamen consumebatur.*

P. D. THOMSON.

Edinburgh
April 1943.

CHAPTER I
THE CHALLENGE TO THE CHURCH

I

PRESENT world conditions offer a challenge to the Christian Church—a serious challenge. Powerful anti-Christian movements are active abroad and at home, claiming to provide alternatives to the Gospel. Those also who are not for us are against us : there are many who are totally indifferent to what we call the things of Eternity. Changes, some of them plainly changes for the better, have produced a new environment in which the work of the Church has now to be done. The message has to be brought to people who feel themselves better educated than were their fathers, or who have at least come within range of new knowledge with regard to the world as described by Science, and who have been influenced by advances in psychology, in biblical research, in comparative religion, and perhaps most of all in economic theory. Fiction and the press have had more effect upon people's outlook than many of them realise. Modern conditions of work and life, absorbing public duties, distracting amusements and a multitude of stimulating and satisfying interests crowd the days and divert attention from religious thought and practice. The Bible is not read as when fewer books were available, and Sunday is not kept as when its strict observance had the support of fear and superstition as well as of tradition. The finality of the Christian ethic is no longer a general assumption. In some quarters there is a new assurance and sense of power as a result of modern discoveries, and a corresponding absence of a sense of need. In others there is a pessimistic depression due to a consciousness that materialistic progress is bringing so little that has real value. And some have made a hasty retreat behind the walls of authority whether that of Rome or, more surprisingly, the dogmatism of some new sect. Fortunately many have been made conscious of various views widely and conscientiously maintained, and are ready at least to discuss. The war is certainly the beginning of a world situation different from anything previously experienced, and thoughtful persons, both within and without the Church are probing the possibilities and earnestly considering the meaning of things, social and industrial questions, the position of women, the place of the family, the principles of education, the nature of the State, international relations, and such-like complicated and perplexing problems.

The Church's working concern is the spiritual health of the individual and the community to the glory of God ; and it can never forget that human nature remains essentially the same through the centuries. It is noticeable that the poets in all the ages and languages have written about exactly the same few subjects. The same old courage and faith that used the bows and arrows and shields of other days are needed for the conflicts of our generation. And Jesus Christ is the same yesterday, and to-day and for ever. Conditions, however, have changed enormously, and to this fact the Church, if it is to be adequate for its task, must respond with energy and consecration. New emphases, fresh methods, up-to-date vocabulary may well be required. Much that was admirable and helpful in former days and circumstances may have to be scrapped. Much that we imagined to be of the very nature of things may have to be abandoned. The battles of our time demand the very latest weapons and armour. The Church must in all humility and with all its energy prepare the way of the Lord for the time that lies ahead.

History offers both warning and encouragement. It is to be remembered that there have been serious challenges before now. Thus the early Christians found themselves constantly faced by pagan misunderstanding : hence the famous Apologies of Tertullian and Origen and Augustine. A Scottish defender of Romanism, writing of the Church in the period before the Reformation, says : " The poor simple people so dearly bought by the blood and death of Jesus Christ, our Saviour, miserably perish ; the Kirk is slandered ; God is dishonoured ; all heresies, wickedness and vice reign." And there is the well-known statement of Bishop Butler in the early eighteenth century : " It is come, I know not how, to be taken for granted by many persons that Christianity is not so much as a subject of enquiry, but that it is now at length discovered to be fictitious." So in one age after another the Church had to face a challenging situation.

At some periods it proved better able than at others to meet the need of the times. Every era produced its peculiar temptations and dangers as well as its opportunities. Sometimes the Church could only witness by suffering. There was direct persecution as at Rome under the Emperor Nero, or in Scotland in the Killing Time when our forefathers endured to the end. It is true that times of persecution may generate in the oppressed a tendency to narrowness, bigotry, fanaticism and unbrotherliness. Some early schismatic movements of the Puritan type, such as Montanism and Donatism and later eccentric sects of the Cromwellian period and episodes in the history of the Covenanters, remind us of the more unlovely walks into which sincere and ardent Godfearers may stumble, and Pharisaism is apt to be one outcome of the very best intentions.

On the other hand, Tertullian could write that " the blood of the martyrs is seed." Trouble tested devotion and brought out the heroic element, and buttressed conviction ; and the world was impressed. As contrasted with such conditions, times of peace likewise presented to the Church both danger and opportunity. They freed men to reflect and mature and broaden ; but they were not without spiritual peril. For example, when the Emperor Constantine began to treat the Church with favour, it did indeed seem to such a leader as Athanasius that Christianity was now finally triumphant. The Church had not only peace to breathe, but it had authority and all the psychological and material advantages that come from official backing, and it could at last bring weighty influence to bear upon public affairs, was in a position to present its teaching and way of life to a vastly wider circle than ever before, and could in fact openly set up the Cross in the very heart of the community. The kingdoms of the world had

apparently become the Kingdom of the Lord. But while much
had thus been gained, something serious had at the same
time been lost. Under peace conditions a period of bitter
controversy began within the Church. The normal spiritual
and moral standard was scarcely maintained at the level which
it had reached in the small enthusiastic groups of the first
Christians. As St Hilary of Poitiers wrote, the Church now
gloried in being loved by the world, " she who could not be
Christ's did the world not hate her." At an earlier date
St Cyprian, after a lengthy period of quiet, sadly pointed out
that " long repose had corrupted the discipline," increase of
wealth had introduced ecclesiastical worldliness, and general
laxity of manners and conduct had supervened. We recollect
also that in the history of the Church of Scotland there were
never more abuses than in the time before the Reformation
when the Church was at the height of its political power and
social influence.

One cannot, therefore, pronounce as to what conditions
have proved most difficult for the Church. The Christian
community, like the Christian individual, ought to be able to
compel every experience to evolve a blessing, ought so to
respond to the challenge of circumstances as to force all
happenings to yield a Christian message and serve a Christian
purpose. There have been occasions in history when the Church
has not been able for its problem, as for example in North Africa
when organized Christianity simply disappeared before the
Vandals, and when later the Christians of various Eastern
lands were unable to stand up to the armed missionaries of
Islam. On the other hand, the history of Missions is full of
instances of apparently insuperable difficulties overcome and
victory wrenched from defeat. And one of the most encouraging
lessons of the past is the extent to which the Church has time
and again proved its vitality by its power of adapting itself
to new conditions. It survived the Copernican Revolution
and absorbed the new learning of the Renascence period.
Protestantism was able to shed Monasticism which had been
the most characteristic feature of the Middle Ages, and actually
increased its vigour through the operation. The modern Church

has adapted itself to Darwin and all that that name signifies. What has resulted in any particular case has under God depended upon the state of preparedness and consecration of professing Christians and their adaptability and fitness to meet specific conditions.

II

For a Church that is to be fit to face the future, one of the important requisites will certainly be Unity. Jesus, according to St John, prayed that his followers might be one that the world might believe. And St Paul exhorted the Ephesians to walk worthily of their calling, " endeavouring to keep the unity of the Spirit in the bond of peace." " There is," he declared, " one body, and one Spirit, even as ye are called in one hope of your calling ; one Lord, one faith, one baptism, one God and Father of all, who is above all, and through all, and in you all." It was with a view to the establishment of Unity in the Church that the Emperor Constantine summoned the First General Council at Nicæa in A.D. 325. It was in the hope of ensuring Protestant Unity that Philip of Hesse in 1529 called the Colloquy of Marburg, where unhappily Zwingli and Luther failed to agree. Calvin felt the need of Unity in the Church, and wrote : " Amongst the greatest evils of our age there is also to be reckoned that our Churches are so distracted one from another." The Lausanne Conference on Faith and Order in 1927 in its report proclaimed : " God wills Unity. Our presence in this Conference bears testimony to our desire to bend our wills to His. However we may justify the beginnings of disunion, we lament its continuance, and henceforth must labour, in penitence and faith, to build up our broken walls."

There can be no doubt as to the evil of Schism. All Christendom still suffers because of the separation which took place in 1054 between the Churches of the East and the West ; in isolation neither the Church with its centre at Rome, nor that which had its base at Constantinople has been able to display the fulness of Christ. The cleavage between Romanism and Protestantism which took place at the Reformation remains a serious hindrance to the cause of Christ. In 1688 the celebrated French divine, Bossuet, published his *History of Variations* to prove that Protestantism by reason of its many sects was " a kingdom disunited, divided against itself, and which must fall sooner or later." James Durham, an eminent Scots preacher and exegete of the seventeenth century, declared that " there is nothing that doth more tend to the reproach of the blessed name of our Lord Jesus, that maketh Christianity more hateful, that rendereth the Gospel more unfruitful, and more marreth the progress and interest of the Kingdom of our Lord Jesus, and in a word doth more shut out all good and let in by an open door everything that is evil into the Church than this woeful evil of division." We have heard of Scottish villages at the close of the nineteenth century with three or four rival Presbyterian congregations. A recent report gave the number of different missionary societies that had been working in China as 132. At the Madras Conference of 1938 it was affirmed that as far as the mission field was concerned the disunity, competition and overlapping of the denominations constituted " a stumbling-block to the faith " and " a mockery to those without."

We may therefore declare that God wills Unity and that Schism is to be reckoned as a deadly sin. Careful discrimination must, however, be made between Unity and Uniformity. True Unity is quite compatible with differences in belief and practice. The first Church members are described in the Book of Acts as " of one heart and of one soul," and that reveals the true test. St Gregory the Great comforted a worried bishop by the statement that " where there is one faith a diversity of usage does no harm to Holy Church." In this connection, while the avowed aim of the Solemn League and Covenant of 1643 was " to bring the Churches of God in the three kingdoms to the nearest conjunction and uniformity in religion, confession of faith, form of Church government, directory for worship and catechising," and " the extirpation of popery, prelacy, super-stition, heresy, schism. . . . that the Lord may be one and His name one in the three kingdoms," we may contrast with this the enlightened phrasing of the Church of Scotland Act,

1921 : " Nothing contained in this Act or in any other Act affecting the Church of Scotland shall prejudice the recognition of any other Church in Scotland as a Christian Church protected by law in the exercise of its spiritual functions."

Toleration may be said to be now generally recognized as a virtue. In it stress is laid upon Charity. Richard Baxter, the Puritan divine, loved to quote the maxim : " In things necessary, unity ; in things indifferent, liberty ; in all things, charity." The tolerant person has a sense of proportion and is concerned rather about what he has in common with his fellows than about points of difference. Actually the various Churches have in common much that is plainly fundamental—creeds, sacraments, clergy, church buildings, the Bible, the Lord's Prayer, and so on. A Presbyterian may heartily sing hymns composed by Romanists, Anglicans, Methodists, Baptists. Bunyan's *Pilgrim's Progress*, Jeremy Taylor's *Holy Living and Holy Dying*, Scougall's *Life of God in the Soul of Man*, are the property of all Protestants. Toleration involves sympathetic understanding and broadminded appreciation ; but it does not necessarily involve complete agreement. Said John Wesley : " Give me thy hand. I do not mean, be of my opinion. You need not. I do not expect or desire it. Neither do I mean I will be of your opinion. . . . Keep your own opinion ; I mine, and that as steadily as ever. . . . Only, give me thine hand."

Modern Ecumenical and Union movements have this as a dominating feature, for they are not ambitious after sameness in doctrine or practice, nor is compromise or accommodation their guiding method ; but rather do they encourage comprehension, wide, inclusive associations of parties which differ with regard to subsidiary matters, but can work together in a spirit of forbearance and goodwill for common ends. The Edinburgh Missionary Conference of 1910 gave a stimulus to such efforts ; and Church unions in Canada, among English Methodists, amongst Chinese Christians, between French Protestant denominations, are evidence of a healthy modern trend. The Presbyterian Alliance is an example of an attempt to improve contacts between near relations for mutual strengthening and comfort. Scotland, the land of so many

Secessions, has now become the scene of the most encouraging of all Church Unions, the incorporating Union of 1929.

Let us here remind ourselves that even serious differences amongst Christians are not necessarily matter for shame. What sometimes passes for Toleration, ignoring or making light of differences, may be mere Indifference, lack of interest, want of principle. It should be noted that what separates is often not the sectarian spirit, but genuine zeal for Truth. The Psalmist reminds us of the difficulty of reconciling Mercy and Truth, Righteousness and Peace. Those who emphasize Charity may grow slack in principle. Those who cultivate Truth may become narrow and unbrotherly. Thus Toleration was roundly condemned by Robert Baillie, one of the Scots representatives at the Westminster Assembly: " this wicked toleration," he calls it ; " this monstrous imagination of Liberty." And about the same period Durham wrote : " Toleration doth either account little of error, as being no hurtful thing, and so there can be no esteem of Truth ; or it doth account little of the destruction of souls." In this spirit Samuel Rutherfurd composed his *Disputation against pretended Liberty of Conscience*, and James Fergusson of Kilwinning his *Refutation of the Errors of Toleration*. We are carried back to St Augustine's advocacy of persecution. As Lord Bacon pointed out : " To certain zealots all speech of pacification is odious. ' Is it peace, Jehu ? ' ' What hast thou to do with peace ? Turn thee behind me.' Peace is not the matter, but following a party." Here we have the emphasis on Truth, doubtless at the expense of Charity.

The Reformation encouraged the individual Christian to read his Bible for himself, and this inevitably led to differences of religious opinion. Men read in the light of their own experience ; but although one result was the appearance of many sects, the process is not one to be merely deplored or condemned. Biology shows that development is in the direction of individuality and difference. Men differ from one another more than sheep or oysters do. At a primitive stage people may act and think alike under the authority of some leader, but it is a higher stage when they begin to think and act for themselves. It is only by attempting to strike out in new directions that development is encouraged. One learns to think by trying to think. That difference of opinion may be found amongst Christians is therefore not something of which we need be ashamed. At the beginning the Christian community found room for both St John and St Paul. The whole Church is richer for the appearance of the Quakers, the Pilgrim Fathers, Calvinism, Methodism. Leaders and sects bring out neglected aspects of the Faith.

The danger is that the particular point which they emphasize may assume with them exaggerated importance, and that this will introduce a wrong sense of proportion, and subsidiary will displace fundamental. It is very unfortunate that when a group of Christians discover something to which they think particular attention should be drawn, they are seldom able to witness for this within the Church and so to bring their corrective influence to bear upon general Christian thought. They go out or are driven out, and become a sect ; and their point of special witness tends with them to take a central place to which it is not entitled. One cannot live on antidotes alone.

Yet even the over-emphasis of some aspect of divine truth may be beneficial to the Church, rousing men to consider and examine, and producing ultimately a better balance. In this way even the heresies have been compelled to bless and to make a useful contribution to Theology. The heretic is not as a rule a wicked or stupid person, but often someone with great ability and enthusiasm, who has been stirred by the presence of some abuse, or the predominance of some teaching ; and who, in the attempt to correct the situation, swings to the opposite extreme and loses his balance. Thus in the fifth century the pious and fervent Nestorius, Patriarch of Constantinople, was convinced that the Christians of his time were drifting into a view of Christ which made so much of his Divinity as to obliterate the remembrance of his Humanity. His righteous hostility to this superstitious tendency drove him to such over-emphasis of the two natures in the person of Christ that he had himself to be condemned as a heretic. It was the discussion roused by such controversies that enabled the Church to understand itself and clarify and define its beliefs.

III

It may be seen that those who separate themselves from the main body of a religious community do so generally in vindication of some aspect of truth, trivial or important. They show zeal for the honour of God, conviction, principle, courage, will; but they may become self-righteous, bigoted, narrow, uncharitable, intolerant. Their opponents will rather bear the ills they have than fly to others that they know not of. These are anxious not to risk losing the existing position with its advantages, what the past has achieved and has bequeathed to them. They are concerned about continuity and will be impatient of those who appear to them to be always fussing about " some new thing," will be unyielding, perhaps ruthless to the extent of persecution, but are more inclined to be tolerant and charitable if they have the chance, though apt to carry broad-mindedness to the point where nothing seems to matter, and to wish only to be left alone. These two directions represent temperamental opposites. Their conflicts occur in all ages and countries ; and they have often found themselves face to face in Scotland.

One important difference which has frequently emerged in Church History and which involves the clash of these two parties has had regard to the relation of Church and State. This was a main issue at the Disruption ; but in some shape or other it has seldom been entirely absent from the stage of history. To-day it is a very living question in Germany, Norway, Italy, Spain, Russia, Japan and elsewhere. In early times of the Christian era the problem was vital and involved persecutions under Decius and Diocletian, and much argument by apologists. Then came a reversal of policy under Constantine, who thought he could use Christianity as a cement for the heterogeneous races of his empire. Later the sack of Rome by the Goths in 410 led St Augustine to write his famous *City of God*, where we find a political philosophy and a theory of Church and State which have had a lasting influence. In the eleventh century the Church had acquired such power as to dictate to emperors, and we have the relationship known as

Hildebrandism.   The opposite view, which makes the State supreme and the Church merely a State department has come to be associated with the name of Dr Thomas Erastus, a Swiss physician of the sixteenth century.   Luther, despite elements in his teaching which point in quite a different direction, introduced in Germany a State church of this type, whose character was afterwards expressed in the famous phrase, "cujus regio, ejus religio."   The English Reformation was to such an extent the work of the secular rulers that Erastianism naturally supervened.   A third possibility was that advocated by Anabaptism and Independency generally.   Here Church and State have a relation of apartness.   The doctrine of Toleration is applied as in Milton or as is required in any attempt to rule a country like India where many religions are to be found side by side.   In America there is no State recognition of any particular denomination.

Scotland has worked out a solution which suits its circumstances, and has, as a result of its peculiar experience, and particularly of the conflict which came to a head at the Disruption of 1843, achieved a constitution which appears largely to combine the values of the different systems, rejecting both Hildebrandine theocracy and the Erastianism that would make the Church a tool in the hands of government, but doing justice both to the ideal of the national recognition of religion and to the doctrine of spiritual independence.   Much has been written upon this extremely difficult and complicated problem of Church and State, as by Grotius and Spinoza in Holland, and by Hooker, Hobbes and Locke in England, while more recently A. L. Smith, Figgis, Laski and Bohatec have attacked the subject from the scholar's point of view.   Taylor Innes has discussed the Scottish position ; an Archbishops' Committee on Church and State published an illuminating report in 1916 ; Professor Carnegie Simpson summarises the arguments in his *Church and State* ; and the modern situation abroad has been touched by Dr Adolf Keller and Dr Karl Barth.   The issues are fundamental and a completely satisfying solution to the problem may not be attainable, but Scotland made a substantial contribution at the Union of 1929.

A great modern has written a book called *History as the Story of Liberty*. The question of the relation of Church and State may be viewed as part of such a story and not least as it has appeared in our Scottish Church History. One hears of mass movements in connection with missionary work in India. Not everyone realises how common this process has been in the experience of the Church. It is very clear in the case of the conversion of England as we have it described by Bede ; and when St Columba began from Iona his work for the establishment of Christianity in Scotland, the speedy advance of the cause was due to the acceptance of his programme by kings and chiefs whose subjects were then assumed to have acquiesced in the action of their leaders. It was only very gradually, as community life became more complicated and especially after education reached the laity, that the individual really began to matter. From the days of the Reformation there has been a steady growth of the importance of the individual, and though the religious attitude of the community has remained fundamental, the characteristic of the modern period has been the development of individual liberty. In our own time this appears to be threatened in some quarters and under some forms of government ; but amongst ourselves at least, and wherever any true approach has been made to Democracy, the individual has stood out more and more from the crowd, and his life has become richer and fuller. This has naturally come as a result of conflict and struggle and trial and testing, an overcoming of difficulties and a sublimation of experience. Liberty has been gradually achieved " not without dust and heat." And the word Liberty has acquired in the process new significance.

The history of the Church of Scotland has been a succession of crises, and of all the spirit-building episodes none in modern times has been of greater influence in the cause of Liberty than the Disruption controversy of one hundred years ago. The two parties that constituted the Church of Scotland then, as at earlier periods, represented aspects of truth which a true Church could only disregard at its peril. What was chiefly in question was this problem of the relation of Church and State ;

and, as a result of conflict and reconciliation and mutual appreciation, it would seem as if the Church of Scotland has attained a position that will enable it, in a comprehensive unity very different from an undeveloped simple uniformity, with all reverence for varied traditions and all the inspiration of an eventful past, in a spirit of broad charity combined with high principle, to adapt itself to the needs of the new world that challenges it, and to face the task of maintaining together the national recognition of religion and the spiritual independence of the Church, and so of becoming the instrument alike of a new order and of a new liberty.

CHAPTER II
OUR SCOTTISH TRADITION

I

THE Reformation in the sixteenth century was a very complicated phenomenon, with economic, social and political as well as intellectual, moral and spiritual causes ; but one aspect of it was the attempt of the world to escape from the stranglehold of the medieval Church. The doctrine of the priesthood of all believers rose from and encouraged a new sense of individual and personal freedom and responsibility, which revealed itself in the Protestant emphasis upon instruction through preaching and the reading of the Bible, the place given to laity in Church government and the direct share assigned to the people in Protestant worship. In Germany and England revolt from hierarchical tyranny led to the domination of secular princes and so to State control of the Church. In Geneva and Holland the close connection between the struggle for political liberty and the religious reformation left the relations of Church and State somewhat obscure. In Scotland the Reformation had to meet royal opposition, and consequently ecclesiastical leaders, when victory was theirs, were in a position of considerable independence, and could assert themselves to an extent that was scarcely practicable in some other countries.

From the beginning, however, Reformed Scotland found room for two types and tendencies. Statesmen such as Maitland of Lethington may be taken to represent the one attitude, while John Knox may be regarded as the outstanding exponent of the other. Motives were mixed, but on the whole it might be said that the former class approached problems more from the point of view of the community, and the latter from the point of view of the individual. The former were conservative, concerned about continuity and order, stability and security, jealous to maintain as far as possible the advantages of the existing situation ; while the latter were profoundly conscious of the seriousness of specific abuses and prepared to take risks in their eagerness to gain what they believed important and desirable. The former were relatively broad-minded and rational and cautious, and had a strong interest in proportion ; the latter, if narrower in outlook, were above all things zealous and courageous and stirred by idealism. The former regarded religion as one of a number of vital elements in the general life of human society ; the latter regarded it as the only thing that mattered, the soul being eternal and all other concerns merely temporal.

Lethington was a somewhat Machiavellian permanent civil servant at the Scottish court, a religious man and a determined reformer, but with a strong dislike of priestcraft, and scornful of fanaticism, overwrought piety and ill-controlled enthusiasm. He could " look through his fingers " at a crisis or a crime ; and his attitude to the religious controversy of his time appears plainly in the well-known characterisation of the enthusiastic schemes of Knox as " devout imaginations."

On various occasions Lethington was in conflict with Knox whom he thought imprudently uncompromising towards the religious scruples of Mary Queen of Scots, for Knox declared all papists " infidels " and " slaves of Satan " and the Mass " idolatry." Maitland was also enough of an Erastian to dislike such meetings as General Assemblies without the permission of the queen, whereas Knox stood out for the right of the Church to act independently. Maitland further attributed to the monarch a position of sacro-sanctity which was endangered by the plain speaking of Knox and his obvious readiness to resist royal authority in religious matters.

John Knox speaks of himself as judged by his own party " too extreme." Although he had a special gift of pulpit eloquence which brought him command of the crowd, he was no mere demagogue, but one who had travelled and been intimate with men of moment, and had been in contact with Calvin's clear theological thinking and skilful practical administration. His aim was to establish in Scotland a Church every detail of which should have warrant in the Word of God, and in concentrating on this high purpose he felt himself driven to use " rude vehemency," to " speak plain " and to " strike at the root."

While the *Scots Confession* makes it clear that Christ is the only Head of the Church, Knox encouraged Parliament to pass Acts against popery, fully recognized the advantages of Establishment such as was given in 1567, and strove eagerly for better State support in the way of buildings and stipends. The Reformation in Scotland had only been possible by the help of such politicians as Lethington, and Knox and his sympathizers grasped at official recognition. Knox declared his aim to be that " both princes and subjects obey God." But, though he did so much for the establishment of the Reformed Church in Scotland and could not for a moment have envisaged any other arrangement but " one face of Kirk " authoritatively organized on a national basis, we find him latterly very restive, and more and more in conflict with the secular leaders whose policy had obtained control of the religious situation in Scotland. The position may be judged from utterances of his own such as these : " So did the votes of the Lords prevail against the Ministers " ; " The threatenings of the preachers were fearful " ; " Take from us the freedom of assemblies and take from us the evangel." In one place in his *History* Knox describes the embryonic stage of the Reformed Church in Scotland, and here we see most clearly the assumption of " spiritual independence " ; and the doctrine receives emphatic statement where Knox in recording that ratification for the Acts of Parliament setting up the new order was sought from Queen Mary and was not forthcoming, adds : " But that we little regarded or yet do regard ; for all that we did was rather to show our dutiful obedience than to beg of them any strength to our religion which from God has full power and needeth not the suffrage of man," while on a later occasion he told the queen : " Religion comes not from princes but from the Eternal God alone."

II

In 1567 when Queen Mary was deposed, the two parties among the Protestants found it advisable to collaborate. The existing ecclesiastical arrangements were given State sanction and recognition, and the Church was established with its Confession and somewhat meagre endowments. " Our sovereign lord, with advice of my lord regent and three estates of this present Parliament, has declared and declares the foresaid Kirk to be the only true and holy Kirk of Jesus Christ within this realm."

In the period after the death of Knox in 1572, we discover two groups side by side in the Church : on the one hand the party of prudence and compromise whose best representative was Patrick Adamson, Archbishop of St Andrews, and on the other hand the party which, under the leadership of Andrew Melville, became strictly Presbyterian. These parties found themselves alternately in control of the policy of the Church during more than a generation. The former held no strong views on ecclesiastical organization, which appeared to them rather a question of expediency than of principle ; but they were conscious that things were not going well with the Church in matters of discipline and finance, and they felt that it was best for the religious life of the country that the Church should seek to win the confidence and support of the ruler and those in authority in Parliament, and not take up an intransigent position with regard to what were, after all, matters of opinion. Under the guidance of this party the Church acquiesced in Regent Morton's scheme of Tulchan Bishops, and in due course yielded to the will of James VI in things ecclesiastical.

Adamson, admitted by all parties to be " a learned man and eloquent preacher," an orthodox Calvinist, translator of the *Scots Confession* into Latin, looking forward to a Union of the Crowns under James, was anxious for Protestant uniformity throughout Britain, and agreeable to the doctrine of the Divine Right of Kings which gave the ruler authority over the whole life of the community, secular and sacred alike. By the Black Acts passed by Parliament in 1584, and by various later

measures, Episcopal Church government was gradually introduced into the Church of Scotland, until in 1610 the shrewd
and persistent king, now securely on the English throne, was
able to persuade a Scottish General Assembly to accept the full
Episcopal hierarchy, and to acknowledge royal supremacy " in
the conservation and purgation of religion," and the responsibility of the monarch for the calling of Assemblies. Thereafter
until 1638 the policy of the Church of Scotland was controlled
by this right wing party, which tended to regard the Church
as a divine instrument of a divinely appointed civil authority,
and believed that the Puritans in their extreme zeal were
abandoning too much of traditional Church practice, depriving
people of some things that had been genuine aids to devotion,
isolating the Scots Kirk from other national churches and
from ecumenical religious life by lack of charity and over-
emphasis of minor points of difference, and depriving the
Reformation Church of a sense of continuity by casting loose
from the Fathers and leaving these to be unfairly claimed for
Rome. Among the leading figures of this party during the
period of its prominence were Archbishop John Spottiswoode,
fair-minded and patriotic, conservative and unfanatical ; Bishop
William Cowper, a cultured writer and a very interesting
preacher ; Bishop Patrick Forbes, an inspiring personality and
a great influence for good ; and Professor John Forbes of Corse,
erudite and pious and liberal-minded, the best known of the
famous " Aberdeen Doctors." In this period Scottish local
Church government, discipline and worship continued in all
essentials as they had been. The bishops " took little upon
them," and their rule was on the whole mild, unexacting and
tolerant, and for a time roused little popular antagonism.
Their Calvinism was not so rigid as that of their puritan
brethren, and there were things which they regarded as matters
of " indifference," matters upon which there might be different
opinions, where in the interests of uniformity one might
acquiesce in any view not contrary to Scripture and itself likely
to edify.

We must turn back to trace the history of the left wing.
King James found himself violently opposed on grounds of

principle by Andrew Melville and other outspoken and uncompromising vindicators of Presbyterianism and spiritual
independence. The enthusiasm of this party gave the Church
the *Second Book of Discipline* (1578), which was confirmed by
Parliament in 1592 and again in 1690, and is mentioned in the
Basis and Plan of Union of 1929 along with the *Scots Confession*,
the *First Book of Discipline* and Knox's *Book of Common Order*
as a document " held in honour as having an important place
in the history of Scottish Presbyterianism." On French lines
Melville completed the ecclesiastical framework by the erection
of Presbyteries, and carried the Assembly with him in the
rejection of Episcopacy, a system which tended to keep the
clergy under government control and which might be regarded
as a possible inlet for Romanism. The party had suffered
eclipse after the escape of James from the raiders of Ruthven
in 1582 ; but in 1592 it triumphantly obtained Parliamentary
recognition for the Reformed and Presbyterian system, and
the spiritual jurisdiction of its courts. The Act refers to " the
privilege that God has given to the spiritual office-bearers in
the Kirk concerning heads of religion, matters of heresy,
excommunication, collation or deprivation of ministers, or any
suchlike essential censures, specially grounded and having
warrant of the Word of God," and the interpretation and
application of this in changed conditions was one of the matters
on which the parties differed in 1843. The king had at this
juncture been obliged to bow to popular opinion as expressed
by Melville ; but he was not long in seeking to free himself
from the domination of the stricter Presbyterians, and Melville
was led to very forcible exposition of his political philosophy,
calling the head of the State " God's silly vassal," and explaining
that there were two kingdoms in Scotland, the external political
organization of which James was chief, and the Kirk of which
the head was Jesus and wherein James was but a member.
Melville had received much of his education in France, and
was profoundly influenced by the sufferings of the Huguenots
under an absolute monarchy, a subservient episcopate and a
dominant Romanism. A forceful personality, a daring and
intrepid leader of his party, an unaccommodating antagonist

" of a salt and fiery humour," a scholar of repute, and a
progressive educational administrator, he has left his mark
upon the Church of Scotland, and a partisan could write of
those days that " the Kirk of Scotland was now come to her
perfection and the greatest purity that ever she attained unto."
A typical record is that " Mr Andrew broke out with his wonted
freedom and zeal." The " two kingdom " theory of the
relation of Church and State remained in various forms
prominent under European Calvinism. It implied one Christian
society organized by the Church with respect to eternity, and by
the State with reference to things temporal, and it undoubtedly
gave the Church the primary position and the decision in any
given case as to the precise position of the line between the two
provinces. King James was convinced that Melville's doctrine
involved theocracy and was incompatible with monarchy :
" No bishop, no King " ; and the struggle for a time centred
round the claim of the ruler to call and to manipulate the
General Assembly, a very representative body which under
Melville's guidance was so effective that it took much of the
community life away from the control of the king altogether.
The dispute came to a head in connection with the Aberdeen
Assembly of 1605. James was obliged to use force in order to
obtain victory, and a number of the ministers were exiled or
imprisoned. After some time in the Tower, Andrew Melville
was permitted to accept a professorship in France, and Scotland
saw him no more.

III

It was not till 1618 that the party showed signs of revival,
the occasion being the Five Articles of Perth which James
induced the majority of the Assembly to adopt. These prescribed
kneeling at Communion ; private Communion permitted to the
sick ; private baptism allowed in case of necessity ; confirmation
by bishops ; and the observance of Christmas, Good Friday,
Easter, Ascension Day and Whitsunday. Such requirements
seemed to the stricter reformers the beginnings of the reappear-
ance of Romanism, and they further objected to regulations

with regard to worship being thrust upon them by the king in virtue of what he described as " that innate power which we have by our calling from God by the which we have place to dispose of things external in the Church as we shall think them to be convenient and profitable for advancing true religion amongst our subjects."

One of those roused to opposition by the king's action at this stage was Alexander Henderson, who was soon to become the trusted leader of the puritan and popular party—wise, grave, statesmanlike and spiritually-minded. When King Charles I unhappily united practically all classes in Scotland against his well-meant schemes of government, and when on the religious question feeling concentrated in the St Giles' riot which immortalized the name of Jenny Geddes, and which made plain the intense hostility created by the attempt to impose by royal authority a Liturgy that had no Assembly sanction and appeared to have Romanist tendencies, it was Henderson who was mainly responsible for seizing the opportunity and organizing the counter-blast of the National Covenant. This world-famous document, first signed in Greyfriars' Kirk at Edinburgh on 28th February 1638, was shrewdly constructed, being primarily a reaffirmation of the 1581 Negative Confession ; and had an enthusiastic reception throughout the country, being thoroughly anti-Romanist, entirely loyal to the throne, finding warrant in Scripture and Scottish history, confining itself in its application to general statements and avoiding controversial details, but stressing the national resolve to maintain " the purity and liberty of the Gospel."

A General Assembly at Glasgow in November of that same year established the complete dominance of Puritanism, and adopted extreme measures against the supporters of the royal prerogative and everything which they represented. The leaders of the opposite faction were deposed or excommunicated. The King's Commissioner had been present at the opening, but when he realized that it was a party gathering and was composed entirely of Covenanters, he declared it to be dissolved. The Assembly, however, continued to sit, the Moderator pronouncing that God " hath given divine warrants to con-

vocate assemblies whether magistrates consent or not," though
it must be noted that the Covenanters so far yielded on this
point as to homologate next year in the presence of the King's
Commissioner the proceedings of 1638, and to accept State
recognition of them.

Samuel Rutherfurd and George Gillespie were typical of
the early Covenanters. They were strict Calvinists, strong
Protestants, zealous Presbyterians, scrupulous Puritans. They
advocated the " two kingdom " theory of the relation between
Church and State, condemning alike Erastianism and Separat-
ism, disputing after the scholastic fashion in bulky volumes,
and basing their conclusions upon the authority of Scripture,
Antiquity and the Reformed writers. It was their belief that
people had the right to choose their own minister, though they
anxiously dissociated themselves from the more thoroughly
democratic position of the English Independents in this matter,
and were content if elders sought out a candidate and the
" major or better part of the congregation " gave consent
" tacit or expressed." Gillespie says : " The States of Zealand
did abolish patronages and give to each congregation the free
election of their own minister, which I take to be one cause
why religion flourisheth better there than in any other of the
United Provinces." Under the Covenanters, Patronage was
in fact abolished by Parliament in 1649 ; and a very strong
denunciation of Patronage occurs in *Naphtali*, one of the best
known of the later Covenanting manifestos.

As a result of actual warfare, Charles I was ready to yield
most of the demands of the Covenanting party ; but they had
no confidence in his future policy, and when approached by the
English Parliament, willingly accepted proposals which, in
return for military assistance, seemed to promise security for
Scottish Presbyterianism and indeed the establishment of the
Kingdom of Heaven in the British Isles. The treaty took the
form of a Solemn League and Covenant which stated amongst
its aims the achievement of religious uniformity and the
" extirpation " of popery, prelacy and whatever was contrary
to sound doctrine, this deliberate intolerance and persecuting
spirit being explained by the reason annexed : " lest we partake

in other men's sins and thereby be in danger to receive of their plagues."

At the same time several Scots went as commissioners to the Westminster Assembly convoked by Parliament, and there shared in the deliberations from which eventuated the *Westminster Confession*, the *Larger* and *Shorter Catechisms*, the *Directory for the Public Worship of God*, and a version of the *Metrical Psalms*. It should be observed that when the Covenanting General Assembly of 1647 gave its approval to the *Westminster Confession*, certain qualifications were made regarding the calling of Church assemblies, and it was insisted that the Church could, " by the intrinsical power received from Christ," meet without the consent of the magistrate. When the Confession was ratified by Parliament in 1690 these qualifications were not mentioned.

The Solemn League and Covenant of 1643 was sworn in the kirks throughout the land, and stern measures were taken with such as sought to avoid its acceptance. John Forbes of Corse had to go into exile in Holland. Kirkton, the Covenanting historian, has extreme praise to offer of the state of religion and morals in this period, and James Guthry reports " a sensible change to the better in men's carriage and conversation." We are told that " the Covenant, which from the beginning was and is the most firm and indispensable oath of God, became at length the very fundamental law of the kingdom, whereon all the rights and privileges either of kings or people are principally bottomed and secured." Scottish national affairs, secular as well as sacred, were now in the hands of the Covenanting leaders, the outstanding layman being Argyll, and the only serious opposition being that offered by the military genius of the great Montrose and the quietly obdurate party left by the Aberdeen Doctors. The country was becoming a Theocracy.

Under the intense leadership of men like James Guthry, however, the spiritual and social standard of the extreme puritan party was becoming increasingly exhausting, and a cleavage in the ranks of Presbyterians made its appearance, the occasion being the Engagement which some of the less rigid made with King Charles. After the execution of the

king in 1649 and the later assumption of dictatorial authority
by Cromwell, we find Scottish Presbyterians in two definite
groups : on the one hand, the strict and narrow Protesters who
supported the Act of Classes excluding non-Covenanters from
all positions of trust in Church or State and insisted upon the
signing of the Covenants by Charles II, and, on the other
hand, the moderate Resolutioners, who presently obtained the
repeal of the Act of Classes and carried through the king's
coronation, and who as a kind of middle party tended after the
Restoration to acquiesce in the reintroduction of Episcopacy.
There were very bitter feelings between these two parties of
Covenanters, and in some parts of the country Presbyteries
split into sections which met separately, the situation bearing a
superficial resemblance to certain happenings in the Disruption
period.   The Protesters contended for spiritual independence,
and in 1653 complained of " encroachments that are made by
the civil power upon the privileges of the Church, in the power
of her courts and judicatories, in the admitting and removing of
ministers . . . these Church privileges being not only allowed
and confirmed by the laws of the land, but founded upon and
consonant to the Word of God."

At the Restoration the swing of the pendulum brought
what we may call the Moderate party once again to power.
Bishops were consecrated, Patronage was restored, General
Assemblies fell into abeyance, royal supremacy in matters
ecclesiastical was admitted, and some latitude in theological
thought revealed itself. The changes introduced in government
and worship were not so drastic as they might have been, for
synods, presbyteries and kirk-sessions continued to function,
and the sermon maintained its central place in public worship
with metrical psalms and extempory prayers. Such moderation assisted the general acceptance of the scheme, but support
throughout the country came from many who had developed
a decided distaste of what they regarded as fanatical discipline,
narrow theology, bigoted self-righteousness and theocratic
tyranny, and who debited against the Covenanters such
incidents as the massacre of prisoners and women after Philiphaugh, the persecuting methods indicated by Guthry when he

complained that "many did take the Solemn League and Covenant from fear, because the refusing to take it was attended both with ecclesiastical and civil censures," and the bitter contendings and the "great heat and fury" of petty controversy.

Although the party now dominant had all the advantages of a recoil of public opinion, it suffered from its association with the undecerning methods of the inefficient government which re-established it. The stalwarts of Puritanism now suffered their turn of persecution. One Act after another gradually made conditions intolerable. Martyrdom was not uncommon. Several hundreds of ministers resigned their livings and manses rather than accept the Government proposals. Those in charge were satisfied that only a negligible number would take this step, and they were faced unexpectedly with the difficult task of filling so many vacant pulpits. The ministers who went out on this occasion had no organization behind them in their exile or homelessness and were not in a position to make a dramatic exit, but they provided inspiration to many who had to meet at least the possibility of sacrifice in 1843. In the staunchly Presbyterian south-west the country people were driven to rebellion and to violent utterances such as the Sanquhar Declaration, and the harshest treatment was meted out.

James Sharp, a former Resolutioner, the clever and ambitious Archbishop of St Andrews, supported the persecution and was eventually murdered by distracted Covenanters. Other bishops, such as Wishart and Scougall, were well worthy of their position, but not outstanding, and only Robert Leighton, who was not typical of any party, has attained enduring fame. The followers were not more impressive than their leaders, and many of the "curates" who replaced the outed ministers were so obviously their spiritual inferiors that congregations preferred the thrill of the Conventicle on the moors or in the glen to the formal unemotional service officially offered in the parish church.

A series of Indulgences which presented an opportunity of compromise gradually brought back a proportion of the less determined ministers, and the Presbyterians were able to begin

reorganizing their party before the collapse of Stuart tyranny
in the person of James II, so that they were ready to make use
of the political crisis to regain their leadership in the Scottish
Church at the Revolution.

The later Covenanters held to Melville's " two kingdoms "
political philosophy, and often quoted the verse : " We ought to
obey God rather than men." John Welch, preaching at a
conventicle, said : " We are met this day in the name of our
Lord Jesus Christ, the King and Head of his Church. These
meetings ye know are forbidden by authority ; but there is One
greater than they that commands the contrary of what they
command, and his command must be obeyed." Shields and
Renwick regarded the hearing of the " hireling " Episcopalian
curates as a sin, and McWard spoke of the king as having
usurped Christ's throne. One of the Covenanting banners
had inscribed on it : " Christ's Crown and Covenant." There
can be no doubt as to the convictions of these heroes of the
Covenants as to spiritual independence.

IV

William III was persuaded that the inclination of the
Scottish people was to the general attitude represented by
Presbyterianism, and an Act of Parliament in 1690 re-established
that system under the guidance of the sagacious and statesmanlike Carstares, afterwards Principal of the University of
Edinburgh. The position set forth by the Act of 1592 was
restored, and the *Westminster Confession* was expressly recognized, but the Covenants were ignored. Patronage was
abolished once more ; but the election of ministers was not
assigned to any wider group than the elders and heritors. The
Church was freed from the high Erastianism of royal supremacy
in matters ecclesiastical ; but the whole plan is evidence of the
admission of the State's responsibility for establishing a Church,
confirming privileges and ratifying decisions which have the
general consent. The General Assembly resumed its ancient
position of authority, but implicitly the duty of calling it
remained with the king. The Settlement was not on extreme

lines, and it was possible for different types to find a place within its framework and to feel themselves true to old traditions. The country generally seemed to acquiesce in William's strong recommendation of Moderation. Many of the clergy on the right were deprived, in part on account of their political Jacobitism, and some of these might later be found in what we now know as the Scottish Episcopal Church. Extremists on the left who were dissatisfied presently banded themselves together as the Reformed Presbyterian Church. But the king was resolved upon as large a measure of toleration as possible, and so in the Church of the Revolution Settlement, alongside of the triumphant Covenanting party, room was left for ministers and congregations of a more moderate outlook. In a communication addressed to Queen Anne the Church of Scotland pointed out that " since our late happy establishment, there have been taken in and continued hundreds of dissenting ministers upon the easiest terms."

The controversy with regard to Episcopacy did not recur. Absolutism passed with the Revolution, and it had been as useful instruments in royal hands that bishops had been supported by the Stuarts, while the Church had found in them the means to that alliance with authority which was felt to be required. Religion also ceased to be an engrossing official concern of States. The Wars of Religion were over. Economics was coming to the fore. The question of Church and State in its old form was no longer a living issue. Ecclesiastical parties, however, remained much as they had been. They did not settle down together too readily, for the one had bitter memories of persecution, and the other was more acquiescent than sanguine about the Church as now constituted. Perhaps one might say that the outstanding characteristic of the one was zeal with liberty in the cause of righteousness, and the ideal of the other charity with order in the interest of peace. The former was spoken of as the " popular " party, and by some as the " high-flying " or " wild " party, but the term " evangelical " was presently in use, the reference being as in the chapter of the *Westminster Confession* which begins : " Repentance unto life is an evangelical grace, the doctrine whereof is to be preached by every minister of the gospel, as well as that of faith in Christ."

Typical of this party in the early eighteenth century was Thomas Boston of Ettrick, whose *Memoirs* reveal him engaged in constant prayer and meditation and bible-reading, family worship and fasting, visiting and catechizing his country congregation, making private covenants and wrestling for the salvation of perishing souls, wary of the ceaseless activities of the Devil and watchful about parish discipline, mandating his " painful " sermons, writing the *Fourfold State*, one of the most popular of all books of evangelical theology, worried regarding " the asserting of the intrinsic power of the Church," zealous to proclaim the doctrine of free grace, seriously disturbed that Calvinistic orthodoxy was in danger, and that " the gospel of Christ is with many, especially of the younger sort of divines, exchanged for rationalism."

Boston in 1700 refers to a distinguished religious writer as " evangelical "; Robert Wodrow in 1717 speaks of the distinction between a " legal " and an " evangelical " call; and a little later John Willison mentions Samuel Rutherfurd and others as " evangelical " in their preaching. Boston calls his party " the stricter side "; Wodrow refers to it as " the serious godly remnant "; and Willison states its position plainly when he writes: " Unregenerate morality will never please God: let man advance it never so far, yet, till the heart be renewed, it is still but nature at best; and the fruit is always sour that grows not upon the root Christ. . . . There is a great difference between morality and gospel-holiness."

After 1690 the more ardent Presbyterians had been much occupied with pamphlets against the toleration of the Episcopalian clergy who remained within the ministry of the Church of Scotland, and whose influence was in the moderate direction. The matter came to a head with the passing of the Toleration Act of 1711. This Parliamentary measure was followed by another which was even more serious for the evangelical party. The abolition of Patronage in 1690 had worked in their favour. Patronage, however, was restored in 1712, and from this political enactment, which was certainly not promulgated as a

OUR SCOTTISH TRADITION

result of pressure from within the Church, but was forced upon
the Church by the State without even pretence of consultation,
arose most of the troubles that beset the ecclesiastical life of the
country in the eighteenth century, and finally the Disruption
itself.

In early days Patronage as a method of appointment of
clergy was not a matter of discussion. There was no issue
upon which difference of opinion could arise. Under the
prevailing social order the landowner was entitled to service
from the tenants and responsible for providing them with
what the standard of the times required in the way of mainten-
ance and well-being. There was no question but that he must
provide a church as he must provide a mill, and he found the
priest as he found the miller. Not only financially but from
the point of view of knowledge, he was the only person in a
position to deal with the matter. In accordance with very
ancient practice the people gave formal consent to the selection
made ; they welcomed the new arrival, but no thought of
personal concern in the choice or payment entered into the case.

Social and economic conditions changed in the course of
time, and in Scotland in the eighteenth century, through the
development of the towns, the whole relationship of landowners
to other individuals had been revolutionized, and the average
inhabitant had some small control of money which enabled
him to say what he would buy or not buy, and some small
amount of education which enabled him to form and to express
judgments to an extent not formerly contemplated. He was
thus building up for himself a new independence, and this
made possible new claims which, when he was able to enforce
them, were regarded as rights.

Apart from this new ability to take a personal interest in the
matter, men's convictions with regard to Patronage were
affected by practical considerations. One result of the
Reformation had been that the personality and character of
ministers of religion became more important considerations
for the people. Religion was an affair of individual concern,
the Bible was a book for individual study, sermons were
material for individual mental and spiritual digestion. Men

C

had now a kind of standard in accordance with which they felt their ministers ought to be chosen.

In 1560 Patronage was associated in some minds with the old ways then being repudiated; in 1649 and 1690 it was associated with the Episcopacy then being dethroned; in 1712 it was associated with Jacobite tendencies in politics and thereafter with corrupt party politics; and as class feeling and independent spirit increased, Patronage became more and more unpopular.

Those who were dissatisfied with the results of the Patronage system naturally sought warrant for their feeling in the Bible, and much was written in this connection, and the opinion frequently expressed that the system was anti-Christian. "The divine right" of popular election of ministers was maintained by such prominent Scots Presbyterians as David Calderwood and Samuel Rutherfurd in the seventeenth century, and later by John Bisset of Aberdeen. Those who preferred to retain Patronage rather than risk the adoption of popular election on the grave dangers of which they felt strongly were prepared to declare such Bible passages irrelevant or misinterpreted.

There was further the argument from history. The opponents of Patronage could point not only to statements of Beza and other foreign Protestants, but to the wording of the *First* and *Second Books of Discipline*, the Act of Parliament of 1649 describing Patronage as "an evil and bondage under which the Lord's people and ministers of this land have long groaned," and the Act of 1690 abolishing Patronage as a power that "hath been greatly abused and is inconvenient to be continued." These unquestionably represented a body of Scottish opinion; and the Act of 1712 which restored Patronage was so far from being sought by the Church of Scotland that it was the subject of immediate official protest as "contrary to our Christian constitution." It was suspected that the Act was framed "on design to weaken and undermine the Presbyterian establishment."

The Assembly of 1715 represented that the Act of 1712 altered the legal position of the Church, detailing various abuses that might arise as, from the non-residence of patrons, the possibility of simony, vacancies protracted for financial reasons, and trouble due to disputes over rights of presentation. From 1735 to 1784 the Kirk consistently passed a resolution aimed at " the redress of the grievance of Patronage." It was also emphasized in 1736 that " it is and has been since the Reformation the principle of this Church that no minister be intruded into any parish contrary to the will of the congregation," and no denial of the principle by the Church of Scotland is on record.

V

As early as 1703 a pamphlet controversy developed regarding Patronage ; but for some time after 1712 the issues were avoided alike by patrons, by presbyteries and by people. A troublesome case, however, occurred in 1725 and others followed ; and the method of settlement by " riding committees " from headquarters to override the local ecclesiastical courts proved to be in the interests of law and authority rather than of goodwill. Then came the famous Act of 1732. It begins by referring to the " grievances arising from the Act restoring patronages," and seeks to restrict the possible occasions of conflict by a method of dealing with the numerous instances in which the patron did not exercise his right of presentation within six months of the date of a vacancy, entrusting the election in such cases to heritors and elders, who would propose their candidate for approval or disapproval, reasons for disapproval to be judged by the Presbytery. This was practically restoring in one set of cases the Act of 1690, and to that extent might be thought to have offered partial amendment and to deserve acceptance. Such a view was indeed taken by the Assembly ; but presbyteries had in practice been going even further when presentation to parishes had passed into their control, for they had been consulting the wishes also of heads of families. Besides this, there was increasing opposition to the influence left with heritors who might not even be Christian. Further, there was hostility to continuing rights in connection with the choice of a minister " to the man with the gold ring and the gay clothing." This definitely democratic side of the case is to be noted, and became increasingly important.

But the main antagonism to the Act of 1732 was due to the fact that it acquiesced in Patronage, and was accordingly declared to " wound and subvert the frame and constitution of Christ's Church, shut the gospel-door of entering the Lord's House, open a window of human contrivance for access to thieves and robbers, and lay a yoke of spiritual slavery, heavier than that of Egyptian bondage, on the necks of them whom the Lord hath made free."

The First Secession of 1733 was led by the devout and determined Ebenezer Erskine and a few other fervent Evangelicals who felt that the condition of the Church of Scotland made separation imperative. They objected, for example, that the Headship of Christ was not adequately asserted ; the Covenants were disregarded ; re-establishment at the hands of the State had been accepted by Presbyterians ; Toleration was thrust upon the Church by the civil authorities ; Patronage was restored by the same power ; ministers were violently intruded into congregations and the people deprived of their right to elect ; the Church had failed to witness against theological speculation, reason and nature being preached to the disparagement of revelation and efficacious free grace ; the Assembly allowed the representative of the State to appoint the time of its meetings, and liberty of conscience to make protest against backsliding was denied to individual ministers. On minor points the Seceders at later dates up to the early nineteenth century divided and subdivided.

The Second Secession followed the deposition in 1752 of the pious and faithful Thomas Gillespie of Carnock, who, along with others of his Presbytery in the course of the struggle regarding Patronage and the rights of the people had, on grounds of conscience, refused obedience to instructions given by higher Church courts. The Relief Church which developed from this incident was strongly opposed to State interference with religion and had some other points in common with English nonconformity.

These movements gradually received a considerable measure

of support amongst ardent Christian worshippers for whom
the Church of Scotland was not providing or not providing
acceptably, and they were early demonstrations of a new sense
of rights and responsibilities which foreshadowed modern
democratic principles. Evangelicals generally were of much
the same mind as the Seceders, but most of them felt that there
was ample scope for the assertion of their convictions and the
achievement of their ends within the Church of Scotland, and
they had distinguished exponents of their position in such
men as Dr John Erskine of Greyfriars, Edinburgh, whose
merits have been handsomely acknowledged by one so little
attracted by the party as Sir Walter Scott.

The policy of the Church of Scotland, however, was, during
the second half of the eighteenth century, under the control of
the Moderate party, who placed law before liberty and authority
above conscience, and were prepared to enforce discipline and
order and the will of the organized community even at the risk
of the repression of the individual and the restriction of rights.

William Leechman, who became Principal of the University
of Glasgow, employed in 1741 the adjective " moderate " and
praised " wisdom and moderation," and the term was in
common use as a party designation before Witherspoon's famous
satire was published in 1753. The temperament and tendency
were in evidence in " the prevailing party " from the beginning
of the century, increasing as a result of the restoration of
Patronage, and as an effect of the type of training given in the
colleges by such friends of reason as Francis Hutcheson, John
Simson and Archibald Campbell.

To the Evangelical the Moderate was a mere " legalist," of
" lax principles," advocating a " latitudinarian scheme,"
producing in the pulpit " carnal and lifeless preaching," " a
harangue of heathen morality " and " coldrife prayers,"
displaying " a pretence of universal charity." " They cry up
charity for these that differ," says Adam Gib ; " Oh absurdity !
they cannot endure that men should agree in anything but
uncertainty, ever learning and never able to come to the
knowledge of the truth." Their preparation, according to a
writer in 1740, is " merely literal and bookish, making an idol

of a book, which hindereth communion with God." They are
" negligent " about pastoral duties, " superficial and formal "
in administering the sacraments, leaving their congregations
in " a dreadful spirit of security, deadness and indifferentcy,"
" desiring more to converse with those that might better them
by their parts than such as might better them by their graces " ;
the young clergy " employing themselves in keeping clubs and
balls with idle, vain company, when they should be employed
in their closets about the study of holiness," cultivating " great
men and lawyers " and " persons of note and quality," too
ready to " show deference to human authority " ; entering the
ministry " for a livelihood in the world " and prepared to
accept a presentation without a call.

The Moderate was inclined to reply by being contemptuous
of such as appeared to him crudely Judaic, living in an unreal
world of superstition, scholasticism and self-righteousness, and
in danger of bigotry, cant, morbidity, vulgarity, exaggerated
austerity, excited emotionalism, and an uncharitable, factious
spirit, their pulpit utterances capable of degenerating into mere
torrents of words, jumbles of Bible phrases, appealing by highly
coloured descriptions and unrestrained tones to the fears and
imaginations of the simple. No doubt extremes in both party
directions were comparatively few. Not many ministers would
have all the virtues or all the defects of their party, and many
might even have proved difficult to assign rather to the one
than to the other.

The Moderate school did something to bring the Church
into line with the spirit of the great age of Reason which had
dawned with the rise of modern philosophy and science under
the influence of Descartes, and which owed much to the rival
Scottish thinkers, David Hume and Thomas Reid. Toleration
and freedom of thought and enquiry were the marks of the
time ; but there was little encouragement to apply such
principles in the sphere of Theology, and we find that the
brilliant men whom the party produced brought distinction to
Scotland chiefly by contributions to literature, history, and
philosophy. John Home, the dramatist ; Hugh Blair, the
rhetorician ; William Robertson, the historian ; William

Wilkie, the poet ; George Campbell, the gallant assailant of Hume ; Alexander Gerard, the essayist ; Thomas Reid, the commonsense philosopher, were amongst the Church of Scotland ministers who made the period the most outstanding for wealth of intellectual production in the whole history of our country. The best of the party were cultured gentlemen, liberal-minded, tolerant and high-principled, concerned for public order and practical religion. Dr Samuel Johnson was much impressed by the character and learning even of those Moderates whom he found ministering in the remote Hebrides. Both the qualities and the failings of the type are revealed in the statement by Miss Mure of Caldwell : " There was still in the country a taste for good morals, which was improved by a set of teachers among us, most of whom had their education abroad or had travelled with young gentlemen . . . those taught that whoever would please God must resemble him in goodness and benevolence, and those that had it not must affect it by politeness and good manners." Characteristic Moderate preaching, as we find it in Leechman, requires that doctrines should have " a real tendency to make men wiser and better, to enlighten their minds, purify their hearts, and reform their lives." Duty and example and knowledge of God are inculcated, and it is emphasized that there is " nothing sour, morose or gloomy " about Christianity, but that it inspires " serenity, peace and cheerfulness " and produces " a joyful and devout society." At the same time, one must not overlook emphasis on Revelation, on the Gospel as Grace, on the genius of Christianity as Love and on the need for the proclamation of the Word to all mankind.

But the pendulum was to swing again. Our sketch has brought us to the beginning of the Evangelical Revival, a period of gradually intensifying spirituality which culminated in the Disruption.

CHAPTER III

THE SOCIAL BACKGROUND

I

IN the second half of the eighteenth century Scotland wakened up and began to flourish. Gradually farmers were persuaded to abandon the ancient run-rig system, to fence and drain the land, and to introduce a suitable rotation of crops, to experiment with artificial grasses and rootcrops, to make proper provision for the winter-feeding of cattle, to invest in less primitive implements, to take a more scientific interest in breeding, to recognize the value of plantations and hedges, and to require terms of tenure which would justify improvements. Conditions of living improved ; stone became general for housebuilding ; furnishings, dress, amusements, music, periodicals, all gave evidence of marked advance in taste and in the means of satisfying it. The Secession Churches witnessed to the existence of genuine concern for the things of the Spirit, and evangelical religion found nourishment in Boston, Ralph Erskine and Willison. An unflinching Calvinistic and Biblical orthodoxy combined with an independent spirit and a consciousness of personal rights and responsibilities that were remarkably advanced for that period. The most astonishing progress was in the realm of thought. The deistic controversy with the fresh knowledge it brought of what the world was thinking under the influence of Descartes and Voltaire ; the famous work of the Scots, Thomas Reid, David Hume and Adam Smith ; and the wide acceptance by the orthodox of the championship of Bishop Butler, all implied that the mind was at work upon the fundamentals with a new vigour and freedom. Principal Robertson's Histories attracted universal notice ; Smollett won a high place amongst the novelists ; Robert Burns brought genius to the writing of Scots songs ; and a considerable number of Scots clergymen wrote and preached with more approach to originality than Scotland had known since the Reformation. In the towns there were numerous clubs, some indeed chiefly for drinking, but many for sober discussion of all topics from drainage to divinity. Glasgow was now a busy city where sugar magnates dwelt in stylish mansions and paraded the Saltmarket with wigs and snuff-boxes and gold-headed canes.

Of the year 1789, John Galt, in the *Annals of the Parish*, makes the Rev. Micah Balwhidder declare : " This I have always reflected upon as one of our blessed years. . . . There was a hopefulness in the minds of men, and a planning of new undertakings, of which, whatever may be the upshot, the devising is ever rich in the cheerful anticipations of good." These words clearly state the drift of affairs and the spirit of a period which was characterized by the Industrial Revolution, the French Revolution, the Romantic Revival, and the Evangelical Revival ; and which we must consider closely as including the more immediate preparation of those forces of which the Disruption was an outstanding expression.

The youthful Wordsworth shared the optimistic outlook as to 1789 ; but there was another view, and this was perhaps best expressed by Burke where with reference to the same eventful point of history he wrote : " When ancient opinions and rules of life are taken away, the loss cannot possibly be estimated. From that moment we have no compass to govern us ; nor can we know distinctly to what port we steer." He considered that the new age was obsessed by a desire for material advance through commerce, trade and manufacture, and that it was prepared to sacrifice to this both culture and religion. That such a view of the direction of events was present also amongst responsible and prudent men in Scotland is shown by the considered opinion of Thomas Somerville, a shrewd Border minister, who came to the conclusion that " the very existence of civil society was in danger." It is important for us to realize the force of both those attitudes to the drift of the times.

In March 1789 light was first put to the blast furnace of the new ironworks at Muirkirk in Ayrshire. Since the opening of the Carron Ironworks in 1759 the process of smelting iron with coal had been greatly improved through the discoveries and inventions of James Watt and Henry Cort. At Muirkirk the moving spirit was Thomas Edington, who had already set up furnaces near Glasgow and elsewhere in Scotland where coal and ironstone could be mined. The industry flourished and coal-mining became a profitable investment and employed rapidly increasing numbers of workers in Fife, Lanarkshire and Ayrshire. The opening of the Forth and Clyde Canal in 1790 and improvements in the steam-engine helped matters, and though there were anxious periods, perseverance in experiment had its reward, and the industry expanded rapidly after Mushet's discovery of the properties of blackband iron-stone and Neilson's invention of the hot-blast, and the beginning of the use of these by William Baird in 1830 at Coatbridge.

The first Scottish railway was opened in 1826 ; Edinburgh and Glasgow were connected by rail by 1842 ; and in the succeeding decade there was a railway-building mania in Scotland. The original purpose of railways was purely industrial, but they quickly proved their suitability for passenger transport. Roads had meanwhile improved enormously. By 1789 a coach ran regularly from Glasgow to London, and in the early nineteenth century, through the genius of McAdam and Telford, serviceable roads and bridges made communication with all parts of the country vastly more rapid and comfortable than ever before. The same period witnessed decided advances in connection with the provision of harbours and docks, the deepening of the Clyde channel, the erection of lighthouses and the building of ships.

The textile industries were revolutionized in this period by the development of machinery and the factory system. By 1789 the first mill for the spinning of yarn for cloth had been established in Scotland in connection with the linen trade. There had from early in the century been widespread and increasing activity in the production of linen under domestic and small business conditions, and there were numerous lint-mills and bleaching grounds ; but progress in the trade was slow. The cotton industry made a more sensational advance. By 1789 this trade was booming. A cotton mill using water-power was built in that year at Ballindalloch, and there were others at Catrine, New Lanark and Deanston. Soon the industry was the most flourishing in the land. Wool had always been well worked in Scotland, and now sheep-rearing greatly increased in amount, with good results both for food and clothing, though unfortunately with the accompaniment of wholesale evictions in Highland areas. The weaver was an important figure in Scottish politics and religion. Not till the middle of the nineteenth century did the handloom seriously give place to a factory system. Meanwhile the weaver had his years of great prosperity at the close of the eighteenth century, followed by an embittering period of decreasing wages and widespread unemployment a generation later. Many accounts agree with the statement of Thomas Guthrie, that the weavers were " great readers, devourers of books and that to good purpose," and we know of the weaver who complained that he could not find Dr Chalmers's " lang-nebbed " words even in the dictionary. In the literature of the time the weaver is generally credited with radical views in Theology and in everything else.

II

Another epoch-making fact which had its influence upon the mind and spirit of those times was the French Revolution. On 4th August 1789 the Paris populace stormed the Bastille, and every throne in Europe shook. In Scotland the American War of Independence had roused some small measure of political sentiment, and after the Revolution in France liberal ideas found expression in James Mackintosh's *Vindiciæ Gallicæ*, while Paine's *Rights of Man* was eagerly welcomed by a section of the people who had little cause for contentment with existing conditions. There was occasional rioting, the Friends of the People held excited meetings at various centres, and Thomas Muir and other Radicals were transported to Botany Bay. The Church of Scotland took occasion to emphasize " the principles and duties of the true Christian Protestant religion and the obligations they are under to duty and loyalty to our sovereign King George and obedience to the laws." A number of landed proprietors and persons with vested interests appear to have turned heartily to the Church out of fear of the new freedom as a danger to social order. On the other hand, the Haldanes were sympathetic to every movement towards liberty, and there was support also amongst the Seceders where democratic tendencies had long been active. Henry Cockburn noted that " there is a good deal of Radicalism in the country, founded on long and absurdly defended abuses, excited by recent triumphs, and exaggerated by distress." Even where there was no conscious approval of the revolutionary programme there was much awakening, a stirring from mere conventionalism and externalism in religion, an intensification of feeling, and men's political, social and spiritual aspirations were all in the same direction. As people began to take a personal interest in the political and social, so they were now taking more personal concern for their inner life and there was more reality of religious experience.

The mass of Scots had no means of political expression. Neither of the parties which alternately controlled affairs had any direct interest in the masses. In 1822 John Frost, the Welsh Chartist, could refer to the Whigs and Tories in like terms as " two plunderous factions who have robbed the people without mercy " ; while a few years later William Cobbett declares : " The Tories rule us with rods ; the Whigs scourge us with scorpions." A Chartist speaker in Scotland talked of the Radicals as formerly like a tail to the Whigs, but now " as the beggar laddie that led the blind man said, We're set up for oursels." A change inevitably came over politics, and Cockburn shows that after the Reform Bill " every Tory candidate without exception is professing popular opinions. In a few years the Whigs will be the Tories and the Radicals the Whigs." It was not long before it was pointed out that the Evangelical party in the Church was in line with the more advanced popular political opinion in scattering seeds of liberty, and one writer, referring to the period, says : " Give ignorance power and it will assail without mercy those established institutions of our country that have been reared by its greatest minds and approved by its highest intelligence. . . . The Evangelical majority are not only playing into the hands of the people, but are setting them an example of lawlessness that is likely to lead to the gravest issues."

Social discontent had been stimulated by unemployment. This prevailed, for example, in and after 1820 in a number of trades. Road-making and similar work was provided for some ; but tumults occurred in several towns, and the military were obliged to take action. We hear of the search for pikes that had been secreted by the more extreme Radicals with a view to revolution. Later, popular attention was occupied by the struggle for the Reform Act of 1832 ; in the burghs there were open-air demonstrations with huge crowds and much oratory, and newspaper discussions, An Edinburgh gathering resolved that nothing would correct the glaring evils of the time save " such an extension of the franchise as shall incorporate the independent and intelligent classes with the government and institutions of the country by enabling them to feel that they are trusted to the management of its affairs and have a personal and responsible interest in their success." The general situation is well revealed and discussed in Carlyle's *Past and Present*. Cockburn declared that " the rise of the people in knowledge and boldness is more conspicuous every moment."

The Reform Act proved to be a victory for the middle classes and not for " the people." Much-needed Burgh Reform which soon followed also turned out to be more limited in its results than had been anticipated. The term " Socialism " first came into use about 1826, and was applied in 1835 to Robert Owen. We have the very serious cotton-spinners' strike with the subsequent trials in 1838 ; and there followed Chartist meetings at various Scottish centres. The religious world was profoundly affected by the political and social and economic situation as represented by these opposing doctrines. In 1839 Dr Chalmers found it expedient to disclaim the advocacy of the rights of the people and to insist that what he upheld was the Christian good of the people. There was indeed prosperity in Scotland in those years, but it was badly distributed and many suffered from the thoughtlessness and self-interest of others, and the Church, though active and interested and sympathetic and ably led, was dominated by the *laissez-faire* economics of the day, and can scarcely be said to have taken full advantage of the challenging opportunities presented by the social problems.

In the early nineteenth century there was a steady increase in the population of Scotland, and this in spite of considerable emigration to England and to the Colonies. At the same time there was a marked concentration of the population in the towns, and especially in those of the industrial areas. Relatively, the country regions were now sparsely inhabited and certain parts of the middle belt became overcrowded. Housing conditions in the rural districts had been primitive, and there was little to regret about leaving an existence not even brightened by the flower-gardens of the English village nor distinguished by what we regard as the advantages of country diet. The unattractive country habitations are described for us in Cobbett's *Tour* and Hugh Miller's *My Schools and Schoolmasters*. A brief account of Drumblade says : " The houses were very primitive ; thatched cottages with a ' but ' and a ' ben ' and a closet between ; the living-room had a clay floor and an open hearth, where peats did duty as fuel without a grate ; the other apartment rejoiced in a bare deal floor, bare, white-washed walls, a deal table and a few chairs, and—chief treasure of the household—a mahogany chest of drawers. In front, and in close proximity to the house, lay a midden or receptacle of dust and ashes, forming an agreeable scraping ground for the fowls." Definite improvement on this standard is recorded in what is said of Dirleton in the *Statistical Account* under date 1836, and *Mansie Wauch* shows that the county town might yet be preferred to the city : " Pleasant Dalkeith ! ay, how different, with its bonny river Esk, its gardens full of gooseberry bushes and pear-trees, its grass parks spotted with sheep, and its grand green woods, from the bullying blackguards, the comfortless reek, and the nasty gutters of the Netherbow." Nor must one overlook the Horticultural Societies and Ploughing

Associations which had become so popular in those days and were an indication of new interest and enterprise.

The town houses of the poor were certainly senseless from the point of view of health, built without thought of sun or air and with every encouragement to squalor, disease and vermin. Many lived crowded together in impossible conditions in parts of what had once been the respectable flats of the professional classes. Typhus and cholera were inevitable. The north side of Edinburgh was spacious and had its private wells and its gas lamps ; but one was nearly suffocated in the stinking wynds and closes of the High Street. The capital in those days is well depicted in Lockhart's *Peter's Letters to his Kinsfolk*. The condition of the industrial population of Scottish towns may be illustrated from Mrs Gaskell's *Mary Barton*. The story deals with Manchester ; but it might have been told of any factory centre. It speaks of dingy homes, want of privacy, the impossibility of cleanliness, monotonous work, monotonous feeding, insecurity of wages on account of illness, accident or over-production, the feeble attempts at labour organization, gossip, drink, the pawn-shop, class-hatred and misunderstanding, conversations in a small vocabulary and full of proverbs and clichés, temptations, ignorance, prejudice, narrow experience and outlook, the consolations of religion and the Mechanics' Institute, neighbourliness and unselfconscious and self-sacrificing generosity. The conditions which factory life imposed upon children may be learned from the life-story of David Livingstone, or from the complacent entry in the *Statistical Account*, that " little girls, between eight and twelve years of age, who before were a burden to their parents, were not only able to support themselves, but had a surplus to assist the rest of the family."

We note the alarming amount of drinking by all classes in society. At a political dinner in 1831 there were over sixty toasts and " sentiments " and the party did not break up till " a late hour in the morning." Sentiments mentioned in *Mansie Wauch* include " Botheration to the French," and " Corny toes and short shoes to the foes of old Scotland." The writings of " Christopher North " are evidence of drinking fashions in the period, and though kirk-session discipline cases

resulting in public appearances were now no longer common,
we read of a man in 1832 who was drunk in church, slept and
snored and fell on the stair, and had to sit in sackcloth before
the congregation on the following Sunday. We hear of
unbecoming tendencies at dinners on the Monday after
Communion and after ministerial inductions, as well as in
connection with business deals, funerals and marriages. The
account of the drunkenness and consequent destitution and
degradation which Dr Chalmers disclosed in the West Port
of Edinburgh was almost unbelievable. Lord Cockburn writes :
" Whisky is certainly one of the curses of Scotland. But in
blaming the people for their addiction to it, we should recollect
that we leave them very little other amusement." Notice must
be taken also of the prevalence of crime, some of it due to the
social and economic conditions, but much to an astonishingly
low moral standard. In 1832 a little girl, not more than nine
years of age, pled guilty as a housebreaker by habit and repute
and previous conviction, entering houses by windows and
picking cupboard locks ; according to the crude methods of
administration of justice in those days, she was sentenced to
seven years' transportation.

III

A sidelight upon the popular interests of the towns may
be obtained from a glance at a Scottish newspaper for the
year 1820. As the year began, we are told, the Edinburgh
streets " were crowded with parties passing to and from the
houses of their friends to give and receive their annual con-
gratulations, and noisy mirth, the usual effect of liberal potations,
was to be heard in all quarters ; but with the exception of
occasional drunken quarrels, harmony and good-humour
prevailed." Paisley turners out of work because of the unemployment amongst weavers are reported to have taken to
making toys like the Dutch. Mr Kinloch, a gentleman of
considerable talents, respectability and fortune, who had
presided at a Radical meeting in Dundee, is supposed to have
" made the best of his way " to the Continent. The New Town

of Edinburgh is showing marvellous improvements in every direction. Scott's *Ivanhoe* is reviewed and his Knighthood is intimated. A great increase in smuggling is noted. William Cobbett has proposed a new method of taxation " quite delightful to the imagination for its patriarchal simplicity and innocence." The population of Glasgow is announced to be 150,000. A premium is being paid for raising flax. " The spirit of emigration from the West of Scotland to British North America seems to be greatly on the increase." The first two cantos of Byron's *Don Juan* are published. The Union of the Secession Churches is formed and the press is of opinion that ' a laudable example has been exhibited which it is hoped will influence the feelings and the conduct of other denominations of professing Christians." The queen's case takes up much space in the papers. A golf-club holds its annual meeting, ' dinner on the table at 5." A coach now runs from Peterhead to Aberdeen so that people may leave there in the morning, do business in Aberdeen, and return to Peterhead the same night, ' dispatch hitherto unknown." There are trials at Stirling and elsewhere for sedition. The appointment of " Christopher North " to an Edinburgh chair is opposed on the ground that he has " profaned the scriptures and our holy religion by parodying the Psalms," and that he is a night-reveller and a blasphemer. A parish minister is put under arrest because at a church parade of yeomanry he prayed for the queen. A scientist is to give a series of twelve lectures on Chemistry, but the course will not commence until after the Races. Sunday School Societies are being encouraged because of " vast multitudes of young people being openly observed on the Sunday evening abandoned to their own control." Advertisements appear for Boerhaave's Red Pill, dancing classes, life insurance companies, the *Quarterly Review*, a society for clothing the industrious poor, cures for chilblains, rheumatism and palsy ; a new book with engravings of the bones of the human skeleton with the skeletons of some of the lower animals ; Dantzic black beer ; a public roup " within the Lemon Tree Tavern " ; black bombazeens, sarsenets, crapes, etc., on account of the death of George III ; elocution, French and Italian lessons ; a book-

D

seller's list including Bibles and Commentaries, Gibbon,
Robertson, Hugh Blair, Thomas Chalmers, Robert Burns
Shakespeare, and Sir Walter Scott ; London patented improved
oval-shape beaver hats ; over twenty brands of snuff ; kelp-
shores to let ; a performance of *Henry IV* ; farms and
beasts and implements for sale ; an Assembly in the Public
Rooms, dancing to commence at 8, tea at 10 o'clock, cards and
refreshments as usual ; and so on.

John Knox shadowed forth an idealistic scheme of education
for Scotland, but neither the heritors who were responsible for
providing the schools and paying the schoolmasters, nor the
Church which had control of the teaching, nor the people at
large for whose well-being the plans were intended, showed
much concern in the matter. After 1696 conditions improved,
and somewhat later the S.P.C.K. was doing excellent work in
certain Highland districts and the Dick Bequest was a godsend
to the North-East ; but in the early nineteenth century the
standard was miserably low ; country schools were the merest
hovels, masters were often deficient in both character and
learning, drunkards or men who had failed in other employment, devoid of understanding of the child mind, devoid of the
least acquaintance with sound educational principles, but with
a profound belief in flogging. Many youthful divinity students
struggled to maintain a little authority over a crowd of children
of all ages. Here and there a man of real knowledge and
personality, somehow unsuited for the work of a parish
minister or unable to obtain the necessary influence, would act
as an inspiration to one or two promising lads and give them
enough Latin to take them to the University. A superior
village schoolmaster of the period is described in the *Life* of
A. H. Charteris. Some of the burgh Grammar Schools were
good, with the advantage of having more money behind them
and more expert supervision. W. G. Blaikie, in his auto-
biography, gives an interesting account of his time at Aberdeen
Grammar School.

There was a religious bias in the education system, the Bible
being the main text-book. Hugh Miller has told how the life
of Joseph gave him his first literary thrill. Barrie's *Collection*

was a common reading-book, and contained extracts, mostly
selected with a moral purpose from works as different as Æsop,
the *Book of Proverbs*, Milton, Vergil, Beattie, Home's *Douglas*,
some reflections about death, a character of Forbes of Culloden.
Latin was invariably taught from Thomas Ruddiman. The
singing of metrical psalms and the memorising of the Shorter
Catechism were universal. In 1834 the Glasgow Educational
Association declared : " The great end of all education is not
the cultivation of the intellect only, but the formation in youth
of right principles, dispositions and habits ; and to this end it
is indispensable that the Holy Scriptures be made the basis of all
juvenile education." Schools were visited formally by ministers
and local dignitaries and suitably examined and encouraged.
The fees were generally trifling. Besides the parish schools
and burgh schools there were private establishments, some of
them well endowed. We find advertisements also of girls'
schools which specialized in music, drawing, French, flowering
on muslin, waxwork, white seam and similar ladylike subjects.
At Aberdeen there was a School of Industry for boys " of the
very lowest class " who were fed in return for labour, and the
education of whom disencumbered the streets of children
" who depended for a miserable and precarious subsistence
either on begging or stealing or both." Education was supposed
to be flourishing in Scotland. Dr Chalmers in 1829, in stating
that improvement was required in the training of divinity
students, reminded his hearers that " of late there had been
a prodigious growth in all branches of popular education."

The standard at the Universities was not high. De Quincey
says : " It is the Scottish custom, through the want of great
public schools for the higher branches of education, that
universities, to their own great injury, are called upon to undertake the functions of schools." There were, however, some
distinguished teachers, and in particular Dugald Stewart,
whose philosophical work brought added fame to Edinburgh
University.

The Mechanics' Institute movement had in view the
education of men employed in industry. There was a craze
for " useful " knowledge. People went in crowds to hear

lectures on scientific subjects. Literature, however, we hear, was regarded as "something which ought merely to be encouraged as, on the whole, a more commendable relaxation than a love of public-houses." In some quarters, on the other hand, we hear of someone being employed to read aloud to a group of workmen—perhaps the newspaper, perhaps, as in the case of Dr Alexander Whyte, the jokes in *Punch*, perhaps something less ephemeral. In more cultivated circles it was a regular practice to have reading aloud in the drawing-room ; thus Sir Walter Scott read Byron aloud after dinner on Sundays. We know with what excitement Scott's own writings were awaited, as later were the parts of Dickens's novels which appealed to sentimental persons like the youthful Jeffrey. Wordsworth was much admired in cultured Scottish society. Periodical literature increased enormously : *Chambers's Journal*, *Blackwood*, the *Quarterly*, the *Edinburgh Review*, gave both variety and quality and were widely read and discussed. Children read Maria Edgeworth's moral tales, *Robinson Crusoe*, the *Pilgrim's Progress, Sandford and Merton*. From biographies such as that of Principal John Cairns, or that of Dr Chalmers, we are able to make interesting lists of books which intellectual people were reading at various dates. Works by English writers were naturally prominent, but French was also well known. Cockburn could say in 1849, "Art is still advancing in Scotland," and he mentions with pride such names as that of Noel Paton. The Professorship of Music at Edinburgh was instituted in 1838.

IV

Romantic Revival was another feature of the period. There had been abundant romanticism in the eighteenth century, the nature poetry of James Thomson and of Allan Ramsay, Henry Mackenzie's *Man of Feeling*, the ballad of *The Braes of Yarrow* by Hamilton of Bangour, the Ossian vogue, Beattie's *Minstrel*, the Cambuslang religious revival, Pietism in Germany, Methodism in England, Schiller's *Raüber* and Goethe's *Götz von Berlichingen*, "Monk" Lewis and Mrs Radcliffe's novels, and the Constitution of the United States of America. But the movement became intensified as the century drew to a close and was the outstanding feature of the early nineteenth century. No one did more to further the cult of the Romantic than Sir Walter Scott. In the year 1789 a correspondent wrote to him in prophetic vein : " One day your pen will make you famous," and by the time of his death in 1832 he had made Scotland famous in a new sense as a home of romance in scenery, incident and character.

Romanticism was a temper which depended upon feeling as contrasted with reason, and was associated with the natural, spontaneous and individual, by way of reaction from the artificial, ordered, authoritative and objective. It was youthful, enthusiastic, imaginative, unsophisticated, sentimental, aspiring. It is represented in the theology of Schleiermacher, in the Rousseau tradition with its devotion to the liberty of the noble savage in the woods as compared with the modern town-dweller in the chains of man-made law, in the poetry of Wordsworth and others of the period up to Tennyson as contrasted with the classical forms of Pope and the Augustans, in the medievalism of Newman and the Oxford Movement. The new spirit showed itself in the pseudo-Highland revival of George IV's visit to Edinburgh in 1822 and the pseudo-Medieval revival of the Eglinton Tournament of 1839. It was evident in the awakened interest in old Scottish literature and history manifested in the start of the Abbotsford, Bannatyne and similar Publication Clubs, with the Wodrow Society doing the same for older Scottish religious documents. It appeared also in the enthusiasm with which McCrie's *Life of Knox* was received and the resuscitation of a passion for the Covenanters. The Romanticism of Scott comes out in his fancy for the Middle Ages as in *Ivanhoe*, for the heroic as in the character of Montrose, for the primitive as in the Border Ballads, for the wild and untamed as in the Trossachs. It was something of the same spirit in religion that laid stress upon the Gospel as contrasted with the Law, upon the inward, individual approach to God as contrasted with the external observances of organized religion, and upon freedom of conscience as contrasted with the restraints and requirements of authority. We find it in the idealism of John Knox, in the conventicle worship and martyr spirit of the persecuted Covenanters, in the *Letters* of Rutherfurd and the sermons of Guthrie of Fenwick, and in the evangelical ardour by which the early nineteenth century replaced eighteenth-century rationalism. The same religious attitude manifested itself in other countries : witness the life protest of the pious Evangelical Hans Nielsen Hauge against the formalism of the Norwegian State Church, and the response in Switzerland and France to the evangelical message of the Haldanes.

V

In 1789 a General Assembly vote in Edinburgh may be regarded as marking the turn of the tide and the beginning of the Evangelical Revival which ultimately involved the Disruption. The decision to be made was not important, but a great deal of party scheming took place and the incident was an index of the ecclesiastical situation. The Assembly clerkship was vacant, and the two candidates represented the two parties. The Moderates supported Alexander Carlyle of Inveresk, whom Sir Walter Scott called " the grandest demi-god I ever saw " ; while the Evangelicals voted for Professor Dalzell of Edinburgh, described by Scott as " an admirable scholar," " deeply interested in the progress of his students." An exciting vote eventually elected the Evangelical nominee.

The missionary zeal which sent Carey to India in 1793 roused the Scots Evangelical protagonist, John Erskine, to make a first vain endeavour in 1796 to engage the Church of Scotland in similar enterprise ; and, though it was not until 1820 that the Church did send out its first missionary, the proposal was an indication of a stirring of Evangelical feeling.

The enthusiasm with which the evangelistic efforts of the Haldanes was received in many parts of the country at the turn of the centuries showed that there was a large public susceptible to this kind of religious appeal. The Sunday School owes much to the humanitarian tendencies of this group. In the same period the Evangelical party did something to encourage the erection of Chapels of Ease to supply religious ordinances for those for whom the rigidity of the old parochial system permitted no adequate provision. These new churches drew congregations of people who were eager for worship, but whose spiritual needs had latterly only been able to find satisfaction in Secession Churches.

The two ecclesiastical parties clashed in 1805 over the election to a University chair, and once again the Evangelicals had the advantage. Leslie became Professor of Mathematics at Edinburgh in spite of every Moderate effort to keep him out.

The outstanding figure of the Evangelical Revival in Scotland was Andrew Thomson, minister of St George's, Edinburgh, who died in 1831. Dr Chalmers gave him a large share of the credit for the religious awakening that was presently to transform the ecclesiastical situation throughout the country. A newspaper report at the time of Dr Thomson's death declared that as a popular orator no living man in Scotland was his match or held so high a control over the popular mind. Mrs Hughes pictures him in the pulpit of St George's in 1824 : " His voice is harsh and his manner awkward beyond all description : he stands in the attitude of a mounted cannon, screws and writhes himself incessantly, and seems as if his shoulders would alternately touch his desk ; he uses notes and speaks with great fluency and devotional fervour." Another hearer refers to a meeting in Glasgow and gives some impression of the effectiveness of his speaking in spite of his limitations : " For four hours the densely packed multitude sat or stood, listening with unflagging interest. The variety in his address was wonderful. Every quality was in it but tenderness—nervous argument, masculine eloquence, skilfully arranged facts, clever anecdote admirably told, playful humour, wit that never missed fire, with the more questionable ingredients of bold assertion and reckless personality."

General interest in religion is shown by Chalmers's statement in 1829 that there were six times as many divinity students as vacancies would absorb. Particularly characteristic of the times is the remarkable amount of space assigned by the newspapers to Church and religious news. Presbytery meetings were fully reported. Special services were always crowded with "highly respectable" congregations. Meetings listened patiently to ecclesiastical speeches of three hours' duration. At Aberdeen Synod on one occasion James Robertson of Ellon spoke for five hours and twenty minutes. Lectures on Christian Evidences attracted such audiences that many could not find standing room. Large gatherings heard speakers on Foreign, Jewish and Colonial Missions and on Bible Society work; and when Thomas Guthrie preached, and when after the first psalm the seats were thrown open to strangers, there was a wild scramble till every corner of the building was filled. The general public was excited by the question of Sunday travelling and other desecration of the "Sabbath." The strictness with which the day was still observed may be inferred from the fact that in 1822 seven Glasgow hairdressers were fined 5s. each at the Police Court for shaving on Sunday. Lockhart has left us this picture : "The contrast which the streets afford on this day to every other day in the week is indeed most striking. They are all as deserted and still during the hours of divine service as if they belonged to a city of the dead. . . . But what a throng and bustle while the bell is ringing—one would think every house had emptied itself from garret to cellar—such is the endless stream that pours along, gathering as it goes, towards every place from which that all-attractive solemn summons is heard."

Mrs Hughes has given a full account of Communion in St George's, Edinburgh, in Andrew Thomson's time ; and Jeffrey, writing in 1824, tells of his presence at a Highland Communion, and of "the long sermon in Gaelic preached out of tents to picturesque multitudes in the open air, grouped on rocks by the glittering sea in one of the mountain bays of those long withdrawing lochs." Lady Frances Balfour has described the service at Methlick in 1837. "There was but one service, at midday, in consideration of the great distance from which many of the congregation came. A long array of vehicles conveyed the whole household, servants and master, from the house to the church, and as the huge lumbering old coach holding six inside, with which the procession closed, was seen to round a certain corner on the road, the minister in his gown and bands emerged from the backdoor of the manse, and crossed the village green to the church ; round which and not in which, according to immemorial custom, the congregation, whatever the weather, were assembled. Lord Aberdeen and his family climbed the steep flight of rough stone steps, external to the building, which led to their seat, and the congregation poured into the church ; while the minister, sidling with difficulty past the old women, arrayed in red or crottal cloaks and high stiff white mutches, who by right of deafness sat upon the pulpit stairs, made his way to that eminence, hung up his hat on a peg therein, and proceeded to read the metrical psalm with which the service commenced, and which was sung sitting. The roar of many hundred voices, everyone of which joined in contributing to the volume of sound, unaccompanied by any instrument, was solemn and imposing."

Other gatherings such as prayer meetings were popular. W. G. Blaikie says of his congregation in the country : " Not only did they crowd the old, cold, barnlike parish church during the regular services, but wherever a district meeting was announced, in barn, schoolroom, granary or cottage, the place was more than filled with a most attentive audience."

In those days family worship showed signs of reviving ; elders visited the sick and prayed with them ; the *Christian Instructor* was read. Considerable humanitarian concern was evidenced by legacies and subscriptions for soup-kitchens, lunatic asylums, orphanages, coal-funds. A crowded audience at a meeting in the interests of church extension agreed that they " must either increase the number of their jails, their police force, their standing armies, or they must have more churches, more schools and more of the means of grace." Not only did people listen attentively, but they responded easily to emotional appeal. Ministers shed tears, and whole congregations wept luxuriously on occasion. Sentimentalism was in the air. A remarkable proportion of the monuments to Covenanters were erected or restored in this period. At public meetings, even on political subjects, speakers habitually introduced Biblical references. Susan Ferrier in *The Inheritance* can make Mrs St Clair, after a long and not at all puritanical residence in France, refer to the Fall in terms which no one of corresponding type would now know how to do. On the other hand, Miss Pratt is made to express the opinion that "a certain degree of religion" is extremely proper, though she is just afraid it is rather overdone. And a newspaper informs us that the people of a certain important Highland parish value theology "as little as the conversations of crows." We must also remember the condition of widespread irreligion which Dr Chalmers discovered in the cities : he was of opinion that a third of the population of Glasgow had no connection with the Church. But eddies witnessing to the strength of the religious current might be found in the eccentricities of Edward Irving and Mary Campbell, the independence of Erskine of Linlathen and John Macleod Campbell, and the revival manifestations which began at Kilsyth. Chalmers could think with some satisfaction of the religious position as a whole and of the activities of the Church in the period 1834 to 1839, and we find him saying : " We abolished the union of offices, we are planting schools, we are multiplying chapels, we are sending forth missionaries to distant parts of the world, we have purified and invigorated the discipline, we are extending the Church and rallying our population around its venerable standard, we are bringing the sectaries again within its pale, and last, though not least, we have reformed the Patronage."

CHAPTER IV
THE CLASH OF CHURCH AND STATE

I

THE Disruption was an incident in the search after Liberty. It was Spiritual Independence that was sought by the Disruption leaders, as by Knox, Melville, the Covenanters and the Seceders. This was often expressed as "the Headship of Christ," and Candlish, looking round for "a suitable watchword," selected the phrase, "the Crown Rights of the Redeemer." The problem raised was the familiar one of the proper connection of Church and State, with the even more fundamental issue as to the true relation of the individual and the community, of Liberty and Law.

To this question of Spiritual Independence the Church was led by a practical problem that arose naturally in that particular period of democratic progress. This was a matter of the rights of the people ; and the party which championed these came to be known as Non-intrusionists from their determination that no one should be given supervision of a congregation unwilling to call him to that work, this being a cause for which support could also be found in Knox, Melville, the Covenanters and the Seceders.

The source of the trouble with regard to the Right of the People to choose their own minister was the ancient fact of Patronage, a matter of controversy which once more takes us back to Knox, Melville, the Covenanters and the Seceders.

The removal of Patronage in the Church of Scotland in 1874 was frequently stated by Free-churchmen not to have removed the cause of difference. They were right. The real point of difference was the doctrine of Spiritual Independence. But Thomas Guthrie was strongly of opinion that there might have been no Disruption had Andrew Thomson's anti-Patronage views prevailed in time with the whole Evangelical party, and especially with Chalmers ; and the plea presented to Parliament in 1842 for the abolition of Patronage declared clearly : " the present troubles of the Church are all to be traced to the restoration of Patronage as their source." Patronage, though not the cause of the Disruption, was thus certainly its occasion.

There were several opinions about Patronage. The Moderate party acquiesced in the system. It was not, indeed, until 1784 that the annual protest was discontinued, but Patronage suited them. Patrons had tended to favour the selection of Moderates as men of better social class or ideals, more culture and urbanity, mannerliness and restraint, less intrusiveness with regard to religion, more latitude in theology, less puritanism as to behaviour, perhaps also more obsequiousness, for one eighteenth-century objector to Patronage said that it " keeps the Church in such a sneaking and slavish dependence on great men." Moderatism was also on the side of the existing social order, and Patronage was a vested heritable right and so a property, and there was grave objection to an attack upon such an institution as likely to encourage lawlessness and threaten all institutions. Moderatism further had little respect for the popular judgment and had a serious dread of mob rule. Even George Gillespie in the mid-seventeenth century, while advocating popular election, had admitted that " a mere democracy is the most monstrous government that ever was heard of." And Dr Chalmers emphasized " the wrong and wayward influences which might so easily be brought to bear on the popular will," " their extreme facility to the solicitations of interested applicants, or urgent and interested advisers," " the wildfire rapidity wherewith a petition borne from house to house and prosecuted with address and activity through a parish might obtain a majority of signatures," " the downright gullibility " of the people, so-called popular elections being sometimes an oligarchy of a few or " the sovereign and directing will of but one individual." Much was made of an election such as that at New Machar, where a vote was taken among thirteen candidates who had preached " against each other " ; and it was alleged that in other cases " the lowest electioneering tricks had been resorted to," and there had been left " a legacy of strife, animosity and heartburnings." Dr Macleod of Morven opposed popular election because " it would abandon the character of ministers to the most invidious test . . . and that test was Popularity."

The Evangelicals, on the other hand, heartily disliked Patronage, and the annual protest against the " grievance " had their annual support. Their position may be represented by the words of Thomas McCrie : " A right which is openly put to sale, which may be bought by a sum of money, and in consequence of which any infidel or rake or fool has it in his power to force a pastor for life upon a reluctant and reclaiming people, is a disgrace to a free country, a foul blot on the character of Presbytery, and a public scandal to religion." On the practical side it was felt that while patrons might present men of excellent ability, these cultured gentlemen often lacked suitability for the particular sphere in which they were expected to work. They and the people were not of the same world : neither could appreciate the other. And some were unsuitable without the culture. The democratic tendency in the political world confirmed the people's conviction that they had rights in the choosing of a minister, and encouraged them to imagine themselves entirely fit to make a choice. One speaker in the Assembly asserted that Patronage was certain to go now that the Reform Act had passed ; and it was said : " The male communicants were as well qualified as the patrons to judge of the qualifications of their minister. . . . They were not such good judges, perhaps, of their literary attainments, but what does it matter to them whether their ministers were good collectors of butterflies or scientific arrangers of minerals."

There had continued to be many harmonious settlements, satisfactory to all concerned. There were also cases where patrons or magistrates readily accepted the people's nominee or allowed them a choice from a leet. There were instances of popular clamour for some unsuitable candidate firmly met by an intelligent patron concerned for the highest well-being of the parish. But there were certainly abuses and the possibility of spiritual injury to sincere Christian folk, and there were petitions and complaints, as from Lesmahagow in 1829, while even the willingness of patrons to consult congregations was at best a compromise and indicated a feeling that the existing system was not ideal.

II

In 1824 a Society was formed under the leadership of Dr Andrew Thomson to buy up the rights of patrons and put elections in the hands of the people. Not very much was accomplished; and after the founder's death in 1831 the Society adopted a more decidedly anti-Patronage attitude. Parliament was induced to appoint a Committee to enquire into the working of the practice in Scotland; but though evidence was heard, nothing definite resulted. By that time the matter had been made a subject of debate in the Church of Scotland Assembly. In 1833 some thirty-three voted for the abolition of Patronage against an overwhelming majority.

Most of the Evangelicals would have liked to be rid of Patronage, but they did not consider that such a suggestion was practical politics. They wished for improvement in the system in accordance with the general popular feeling; but most regarded Patronage itself as an inevitable if unfortunate accompaniment of the blessings of Establishment. Dr Chalmers in particular was not prepared at this period, nor for long afterwards, to support the attempt to abolish Patronage, and the subject was carefully avoided by both the *Claim of Right* and the Convocation.

There was, of course, the desire not to alienate the land-owning class; there was the serious doubt as to whether popular election would really be better; but there was the additional complication of the existence of the Secession Churches which were strongly opposed to Patronage but at the same time opposed to Establishment. The challenge of the Secession Churches was one of the causes of the Disruption. The first step to Presbyterian re-union in Scotland took place in 1820 when the United Secession Church was formed; and a further important stage was to be reached in 1847 when this body joined with the Relief Church and so brought into being the United Presbyterian Church with no fewer than 518 congregations. These dissenting charges were not planted according to any territorial scheme, but wherever there was a group of worshippers prepared to pay for the building of a church and the stipend of a minister. They had naturally the privilege of appointing a minister for themselves, and were extremely hostile to Patronage. Ebenezer Erskine and the first Seceders were dissatisfied with much more in the Church of Scotland than the practice of Patronage ; but, in Dr J. R. Fleming's phrase, this was " the root evil which they attacked." The Second Secession of 1761 was quite as keenly concerned with this same objection. Indeed, one reason why the thorough anti-Patronage position was not more popular amongst Evangelicals within the Church of Scotland was just its association with the Secessions.

Those who attended these churches were mostly persons keen enough about religion to be willing to make sacrifices for the support of ordinances ; and as they paid their own way they felt free and independent. At the same time they could scarcely avoid some annoyance that members of the Church of Scotland had no corresponding burdens to bear, and pointed out that what one obtains for nothing is seldom appreciated. It was, however, only in 1829 that the full Voluntary position came to be taken as a result of a sensational sermon preached by one of their leaders denouncing the State connection. This began the Voluntary Controversy which played its part in creating the situation that made the Disruption inevitable. The Church accommodation question had for some time been causing anxiety, especially in industrial districts. Andrew Thomson had said : " Long have we slept in all the pomp of our civil establishment, while in our fields other sects have been reaping a plenteous harvest." Only the Churches of the Secession tradition were, indeed, providing ordinances for the new population. They were offering a pure Evangel, and they could give full status to minister and congregation as the Church of Scotland with its inelastic system was powerless to do, and the selection of the pastor was left to the people ; but they were not approaching the problem as Chalmers and his friends wished it to be approached, for they only built a church where there was a demand for it, instead of supplying ordinances wherever a population provided a mission field, an urgent requirement which the Church of Scotland Evangelicals were convinced could only be faced by a Church that was established and endowed. The erection of churches was seriously undertaken by the Church of Scotland; but when Government was approached with a view to endowment the application was opposed by the Voluntaries, and opposed so effectively that in spite of all the London eloquence of Dr Chalmers nothing could be done, and endowment had ultimately to be provided by voluntary methods.

The need of the new times was clamant and the Church of Scotland was not in a position to meet the need, but the Evangelical leaders were satisfied that with certain important readjustments the Church could become exactly what was required. In the existing circumstances some popularization of arrangements was essential, and one obvious practical step was to produce a measure that, while doing justice in the matter of rights to patron and presbytery, would satisfy the people. In 1832 we find those who were not prepared to suggest the abolition of Patronage, but who were concerned about the difficulties of the times, beginning to use the word non-intrusion, and the Evangelical party soon came to be known as the Non-intrusion party. The expression pointed back to the *Books of Discipline*, but turned attention from the " presentation " to the " call." The General Assembly of 1782 had declared the " call " to be " agreeable to the immemorial and constitutional practice of this Church." The people's voice in connection with the appointment of a minister had customarily found expression in this paper signed by their representatives. The consideration of this " call " had been a regular part of the Presbytery's procedure before they agreed to an induction. The precise legal significance of this document in relation to Patronage was a subject of controversy. Dr William Robertson and his Moderate friends were accustomed to treat it as a mere polite form of concurrence. Ebenezer Erskine, and

Evangelicals generally, regarded it as of the essence of the relation between minister and congregation. There can be no doubt that under Patronage very little attention had for a long time been paid to the number of those whose signatures appeared on a " call " ; but now it seemed to many that the best solution to the problem created by the existence of Patronage and the increasing strength of the movement in favour of popular rights would be the restoration of the " call " to what they believed to have been its original place of decisive importance. Democratic feeling was a relatively modern development, and the people had in fact manifested very little interest in connection with elections before the period of the First Secession ; but there was a historical basis to work upon, and the prospects of increasing the spiritual efficiency and effectiveness of the Church seemed good.

III

It was in 1834 that the Evangelical party at last secured a majority in the General Assembly and passed the Veto Act. This Act declared that it is a fundamental law of this Church that no pastor shall be intruded on any congregation contrary to the will of the people, and that to give effect to this principle " if at the moderating in a call to a vacant pastoral charge the major part of the male heads of families, members of the vacant congregation and in full communion with the church shall disapprove of the person in whose favour the call is proposed to be moderated in, such disapproval shall be deemed sufficient ground for the Presbytery rejecting such person, and that he shall be rejected accordingly."

The Act was not directed against Patronage, but against the intrusion of unsatisfying ministers. Those who projected the measure were, generally speaking, not of opinion that popular election was desirable, though prepared to concede something to the trend of the times, and thoroughly convinced of the iniquity of any appearance of imposing upon parishioners a spiritual leader whose election was repugnant to them. They heartily believed in the Establishment and tolerated Patronage

E

as practically a constituent element in such an arrangement, and
they merely set out to remove features of recent practice which
were rendering the system distasteful and driving Church of
Scotland people into the ranks of the dissenters.   The Act
seemed the most promising line of action at the moment.   Other
possible courses had suggested themselves to leading churchmen.
Dr Chalmers, for example, had thought that the " call " could
be resuscitated by a number of decisions of Assembly undoing
decisions of the court which had gradually reduced the " call "
to a formality.   He also thought that in any case Parliament
should be asked to legislate on the matter concurrently with the
Church.   The political situation was not favourable, and
eventually Chalmers came round to think that " the majority
of dissentient voices should lay a veto on every presentation."
The Veto Bill was moved in General Assembly by an expert
lawyer.   Other legal authorities gave explicit approval to the
measure, and even the Government's law advisers committed
themselves in its favour.   It was understood to amount to no
more than a revival of old Scottish practice, and the Government
actually began to exercise Crown patronage in accord with the
new Assembly Act.

The Veto had its opponents.   Those who were thoroughly
hostile to Patronage denounced it.   They did not want the
existing system to be improved : they wished it to be replaced.
The Moderates voted against it.   They had no desire to yield
lightly to popular clamour, and doubted whether the most
acceptable candidate was likely to be the most edifying minister.
They felt that the Act constituted an abridgement of the civil
rights of patrons, and was therefore both an attack on property
and an infringement of the functions of the State and would
consequently bring the Church into conflict with the patrons
and might embroil it with the Government.   They declared the
Veto an innovation because of the negative form by which
it was distinguished from the customary positive " call."   It
seemed to them that the Act would be a cause of friction in
parishes and of long vacancies on account of disputes between
patrons and people.   It was also pointed out that the Act
deprived the Church courts of part of their constitutional

right of collation or deciding finally whether the presentee
was qualified, and handed over this function to the people or
even to a small part of the congregation who were heads of
families on the Communion roll.

This last point was stressed by Professor Duncan Mearns
of Aberdeen, a learned and able and orthodox preacher, a
clear and incisive speaker and a man of strong Christian
character, to whom Rabbi Duncan has put on record his great
personal debt, warmly recalling in particular his prayers and
his lectures on Christian Evidences. The Church courts,
Mearns held, had since 1567 had the last word in connection
with the election of ministers ; the patron had specified rights
of his own ; and the people were entitled to express their
assent to the admission of the presentee or dissent with reasons
to be judged of by the Church judicatories. The legal and proper
position, he maintained, was as admitted by Moncrieff to have
been the rule in 1690, that the person nominated was proposed
to the congregation " who might approve or disapprove for
reasons shown and substantiated, but who had no power of
rejection without substantiating reasons which the Presbytery,
and on appeal the superior courts, were to pronounce
sufficient ; at whose judgment and by whose determination the
calling and entry of a particular minister is to be ordered and
concluded."

The Act was passed ; but trouble soon followed. In
October 1834 Robert Young, a probationer, was presented to
the Perthshire parish of Auchterarder by the patron, the Earl
of Kinnoull. His spiritual, moral and intellectual qualifications
were not questioned, and all accounts agree that after the
dispute died down, he proved a faithful minister and acceptable
to a large body of the parishioners ; but Dr John Cunningham
reports that " he had none of the gifts of the popular preacher.
He was, moreover, slightly lame in one leg, and slightly
contorted in one hand." His chief defect, however, was that he
was the nominee and nephew of the unpopular factor. The
newly passed interim Veto Act offered to the people for the
first time the right to resist a presentation, and all the discussion
that had been going on with regard to the rights of the people

in connection with the Reform Act of 1832 encouraged them
to make full use of their opportunity, only two heads of families
along with the factor signing the " call," and 287 out of a
possible 330 heads of families recording their Veto against him.
It is obvious that such general hostility, however caused, would
very seriously militate against the spiritual usefulness of a
presentee, and that it was expedient that someone else be
appointed in his stead. That, however, does not in any way
affect the legal side of the matter, and it was this question as
to the state of the law which now emerged. The further issue
as to whether the law could be regarded as satisfactory or ought
to be changed naturally arose later. The Presbytery soon had
the guidance of both Synod and General Assembly with regard
to the course to be followed, and rejected the presentee ; but
he raised an action in the Court of Session on the ground that,
as he had been legally presented the Presbytery were bound,
according to law as determined by Parliament at various dates
since the Reformation, to take him on trials for Ordination,
that is, examine his qualifications for the Ministry. The Veto
Act prevented the Presbytery from going so far as this, and
therefore from being in a position to form any opinion as to
whether or not he was qualified.

The speeches of the distinguished advocates and learned
judges at the trial fill two substantial volumes. A multitude
of legal points were raised ; much research into historical
documents was involved ; and the problem before the Court
was so intricate and difficult that the Lords of Session were
eventually divided in opinion, five voting for the supporters
of the Veto Act and eight for the presentee. The majority
decision was that the Presbytery ought not to have allowed the
Veto to interfere with their statutory duty of making trial of
the candidate's qualifications before rejecting him. In short,
the Veto Act was declared illegal. It was an Assembly Act.
Within a certain sphere the Assembly was indeed a statutory
court, and with its decisions within that sphere no law court
would presume to interfere ; but in this case the Act affected
civil rights, and with regard to these the Assembly had no
authority to legislate, such rights having been established

by Act of Parliament and being therefore only modifiable by Parliament. It had exceeded its rights and entered into the province of the State. In order to make the Act valid in so far as it involved the civil rights of the presbytery, the patron and the presentee, the Church would require to have sought the concurrence of Parliament.

The historical position of the " call " was naturally one of the main points discussed. The view of the Non-intrusionists was that the " call " was a necessary element in every settlement, and though not mentioned in the Act of 1592 or other statutes had always been required by the Church in connection with its undoubted right of collation, and what was within the province of the Church could be regulated by the Church. The Veto Act they thought of as such a regulation and as merely providing a revival of the customary " call " in a negative form. Ordination and induction were spiritual acts, and everything connected with them should be regarded as within the sphere of the Church, and there should be no interference from the civil authorities. Cases were mentioned where Presbyteries for one reason or another had judged a " call " to be insufficient and where their action had not afterwards been disputed. The other party held that though at some periods considerable deference had been paid to the popular " call," it had for long been evident that this was not really compatible with Patronage, and that as long as Patronage remained the " call " could only persist as a form. The revived interest in the " call " was a part of the contemporary democratic movement, which they believed to have very dangerous possibilities. One Evangelical speaker proclaimed that his party " were fighting the battles of the people," and that " what they wanted was to put it out of the power both of the patron and the presbytery to injure the people." There was frequent reference to " the scriptural rights of the people " ; and we find Moderatism later identified in the pages of the *Witness* with unsound doctrine and contempt for the people. These avowedly democratic leanings alarmed the Moderate party. Dr Cook, for instance, deprecated certain action as likely to set " an example of resistance to the law of the land which

tends to the subversion of social order by implying that every
individual may judge for himself when he will obey that law."

An interesting feature of the Evangelical case was the view
that a candidate could not be considered by a Presbytery to be
" qualified " if he were unacceptable to the congregation, and
that this was indeed the point of the " call," a purely
ecclesiastical transaction, not interfering with any civil rights,
but within the competence of the body which admittedly had
authority to declare on the matter of " qualification." Some of
the Moderates were prepared to accept this interpretation ;
but the House of Lords explicitly rejected the line of argument
and ruled that " qualification " referred only to life, literature
and doctrine.

It was also asserted by the Evangelicals that the Church
had always had the right of judging whether the signatures to
a " call " were sufficient and of such a character as to justify
the presbytery in taking the presentee on trials, presentees
having on occasion been rejected in such circumstances. There
was no rule as to the number of signatures that might be said
to constitute a valid " call " ; but the decision in each case lay
with the Presbytery, and had been made by that court without
objection raised by patron or presentee. The " call " had
indeed fallen into practical abeyance, but the Church could
now insist upon making some regulation as to numbers.

IV

The Auchterarder decision marked the point where the
interest shifted from the problem of Non-intrusion to that of
Spiritual Independence. The Veto Act was passed on the
assumption of a political philosophy like that of Andrew
Melville, a " two kingdom " theory, a belief in co-ordinate
jurisdiction. The extreme theory on the opposite side was
Erastianism, a belief in what Laski calls a " unitary " State
which may give recognition to groups by " concession," or
might take the more recent " totalitarian " attitude. A view
tending in this direction was commoner among the lawyers
than in any section of the Church. The Moderate was anxious

chiefly about the difficult problem of delimitation of sphere if one accepted a " two kingdom " position. He certainly feared any arrangement which would give the Church such independence as to say what was within its sphere and what was not, for this would lead in the direction of theocracy or Hildebrandism. It appeared to him that someone must have the final word and that the Legislature ought to have it, though admittedly there might be cases of conscience which would cause difficulty. The arrangement which the Evangelicals preferred was that each should decide for itself the extent of its responsibilities, but this, though it is to-day the accepted position, would seem to involve much of the old possibility of misunderstanding. To-day, indeed, the Church accepts recognition from the State but insists that it does not need it, and we are reminded that A. T. Innes once said : " It was the manner of the Church in Scotland then and always to take all the recognition it could get, to demand more, and to protest that it had full original rights apart from any recognition at all."

By the Assembly of 1838 considerable excitement had arisen, and Dr Robert Buchanan, later to be the chief narrator of events from the Evangelical standpoint, a trusted counsellor and an eloquent speaker, set in the forefront the exalted conception of the " sole headship of the Lord Jesus Christ " and the inspiring doctrine of spiritual independence with all the associations which that phrase brought down from Reformation and Covenanting days. He stated that the question was not now whether the measure had been wise, but whether it had been competent. It was also made clear that the Evangelical party, now dominant, would tolerate no disobedience to the will of the Church on the part of ministers who had sworn at Ordination to submit themselves to the discipline and government of the Church and never directly or indirectly endeavour the prejudice or subversion of the same.

The leader of the opposition was Dr George Cook, minister at Laurencekirk, who headed the Moderates till his death in 1845. He was already an old man, but distinguished by " shrewdness, self-possession and good-sense," " eminently skilful as a debater," " thoroughly a man of business," " author of a very sensible history of the Scottish Church." Claiming to believe in spiritual independence and to be no Erastian, he declared his view that it is incumbent on those attached to an Established Church " to yield obedience to existing laws."

The Assembly of May 1839 followed shortly upon the decision of the House of Lords on the Auchterarder appeal, a decision confirming the Scottish judgment. Ministers all over the country had meanwhile been discussing the issue at Presbyteries, and elders had been taking an increasing interest in attendance at these courts and in the disputations on the existing situation. The two parties were very distinct in most Presbyteries, though they did sometimes shade over into one another, and there were a number whom it was difficult to label and whose reaction to the crisis remained uncertain. Presbyteries had been in the habit of electing their representatives to the General Assembly on a principle of rotation ; but in 1839 we find many cases of definite party voting, and both ministers and elders being selected by the majority of the court because of the specific views they held upon the matters that would be before the Assembly.

It was a very strained and agitated Assembly, sometimes awed, sometimes stormy. The seriousness of the ecclesiastical situation was beginning to be realized. The atmosphere in the crowded Tron Kirk was electric. On the main issue three motions were made, a mediating proposal by Dr Muir being first eliminated, and the motion by Dr Chalmers being carried as against that of Dr Cook. The latter took the view that as the Veto Act had been declared to infringe upon civil rights and therefore to be illegal, it should simply be ignored, and former practice in the method of electing ministers automatically resumed. At the same time he emphasized the " undoubted privilege of parishioners to state, at the moderation of the call, any relevant objections " ; and he added to his motion a clause to the effect that the suitability of a presentee for the particular parish proposed for him should be taken into consideration by the presbytery.

To Dr Chalmers was committed the task of proposing the

Evangelical party motion. He had at first printed his opinion that the Church should rescind the Veto Act ; but he had now moved to another position, and this he set forth in a speech which took him three hours to read and which was marked by all his characteristic vehement and moving oratory. His anxiety was to preserve the " inestimable benefits of a national establishment," admittedly in the gift of the State, while at the same time maintaining what was not within the province of the State, the " great constitutional principle of Non-intrusion." He touched the real centre of opposition when he assured the nobles and gentlemen that " never, never was there a greater misconception than to look on the doings of our Church as they would on the fermentation of some coming anarchy which is to go forth and desolate the land." The Church's demand was totally different from " those demands which are lifted up in the loud accents of turbulence and menace for the extension of their rights as citizens." Chalmers was no radical, and he knew how greatly fear of radicalism in politics was influencing the religious situation. He believed that the House of Lords decision completely destroyed the " call " in any form, and left only a choice between complete Erastianism and complete Voluntaryism, which at that moment he viewed with equal horror. The word " Disruption " was used in this speech —the disruption of the Church from the State. His motion abandoned to the presentee at Auchterarder the benefice or emoluments and proposed a Committee to consider how the harmony between the Church and State could be preserved and to confer with the Government on the whole matter. The Veto Act, which in practice had been working quite well, as even its opponents allowed, was suspended, and all disputed cases ordered to be referred to the Assembly.

V

The ecclesiastical issue in Scotland was definitely affected by the accident of the political situation at the moment. Under Radical pressure the Whig party had carried through such epoch-making changes as the Reform Act and the Abolition of

Slavery; but they were no longer united and decided in policy. In May 1839 they gave way to a Tory party far from eager for office and far from dominant in the House of Commons. Peel was unable to accommodate himself to the wishes of the young queen, and Melbourne returned insecurely to leadership, maintaining his position precariously till a General Election in 1841 put the Tories solidly in power with Sir James Graham as Home Secretary and in charge of Scottish affairs.

After the 1839 Assembly a deputation interviewed Melbourne ; but Chalmers thought the premier's reaction to the crisis " feckless and fushionless," and Tory opinion was strong that the situation would, unhappily for Scotland, be used to build up Voluntaryism. Sir James Graham was convinced that the majority in the Scottish Church were playing into the hands of the ecclesiastical Voluntaries and the political Radicals. Chalmers was himself a Tory, but had written reassuringly to Graham in June 1839 : " Conservatism has nothing to fear, but everything to hope, from giving the people a greater interest and share than heretofore in their church and their clergy. It may create a little parochial effervescence here and there, but we may rest assured that the whole of the ecclesiastical influence brought to bear upon the masses, whom we shall attach to the Establishment, will be on the side of peace and loyalty. Whereas a Church exclusively in the hands, and under the uncontrolled patronage, of the upper classes, will in the present state of the public mind fall to pieces in a very few years." He did not succeed in removing existing fears, for Graham wrote to him later in the year : " It grieves me that at a moment of great danger arising from demo-cratic excitement, fresh impulse should be given to the movement by proceedings which receive your sanction." He could be no party to a measure by which he believed " the right of patronage is virtually transferred to a variable and irresponsible multitude, whose votes are not to be challenged even on cause shown."

A deputation in the spring of 1840 made no further headway with the Whig Government, and pamphlet warfare and heated discussions and bitter attacks rendered a peaceful solution to the difficulties ever more unlikely. There was a widening of the gulf between the Evangelicals and the Moderates ; between (to use Lord Aberdeen's expression) " the fanatical zealots " on the one hand and " the harsh and stern men of the world " on the other.   Dr Chalmers altered his opinion repeatedly ; even Candlish changed his mind ; and solutions which might have been accepted if suggested at one stage in the controversy were later rejected with scorn.   Dr Beith says distinctly of 1843 : " What would have satisfied us a year or two earlier would not do so now " ;   and Lord Cockburn could write : " I consider it nearly certain that these claims might have been adjusted, and even without much difficulty, if either the Whig or the Tory Government had interfered sincerely and intelligently in due time."   But the parties became so widely sundered as almost to substantiate the statement of Hugh Miller : " We have but one Bible and one Confession of Faith in our Scottish Establishment, but we have two religions in it ; and these, though they bear exactly the same name and speak nearly the same language, are yet fundamentally and vitally different."

Of the multitude of pamphlets the best was the *Letter to Lord Brougham*, whose excellent journalistic controversial style brought Hugh Miller to notice and turned the Cromarty stone-mason into the uniquely successful editor of the *Witness* which began in 1840 as the Evangelical party newspaper. One of the letter's main contentions was that not property but moral and spiritual capacity should qualify for a voice in politics, and that similarly the Christian people of Scotland were competent to judge of the requisites of a Gospel minister. It was fundamentally the spirit of religious liberty that had produced the claim to political independence. Miller was on the side of progress. Was it not in accordance with the high destiny of the species that the fit and the right should triumph over the established ? Popular election was responsible for the choice of John Bunyan, Richard Baxter and Thomas McCrie. Christianity was essentially a popular religion. The re-introduction of Patronage was " no unessential portion of a deep and dangerous conspiracy against the liberties of our country." To drive out the Evangelicals would destroy the

Scottish Establishment, and thereafter the Anglican Church would not long survive and the fall of monarchy would speedily follow. The pamphlet is very severe against the Moderates, who are termed " patronage-courting clergymen, practically unacquainted with the religion they profess to teach," whose utterances have " all the cold inefficacy of an artificial religion." Patronage Miller regarded as " the thraldom of a degrading law, the remnant of a barbarous code."

Dr Guthrie gave it as his opinion that Miller " was beyond all doubt and controversy, with the exception of Dr Chalmers, by much the greatest man of all who took part in the Ten Years' Conflict." One of the most interesting brief accounts is by W. G. Blaikie : " The *Witness* appeared twice a week, on Wednesdays and Saturdays. Not many numbers had come out before it became obvious that Miller had brought his hammer and chisel with him from Cromarty, and had contrived to arm his pen with the weight of the one and the sharpness of the other. As regards culture, it was manifest that no existing editor or newspaper writer could wield the English language with half his force or grace. His knowledge of history, his acquaintance with the English classics, his store of anecdote, his familiarity with science, were not only marvellous, but he seemed at once to be able to recall whatever was most suitable for the occasion, and in the use of it, hit the nail most neatly and firmly on the head." Principal Story, from a different point of view, says that he " wielded as a controversialist a strong, coarse, unscrupulous pen."

On the other side, at this early period of the conflict, the pamphlet which attracted most attention was the *Letter to the Lord Chancellor*, by John Hope, Dean of Faculty, and afterwards a distinguished judge—" our high-pressure Dean," as Cockburn labels him—who was as responsible as anyone for the prominence of the law courts throughout the whole controversy, and for the direction of thought that prevailed in legal circles. Both the clear-headed lawyer Alexander Dunlop and the eloquent Chalmers published replies to his pamphlet. It was over-lengthy, ill-arranged, repetitious and obscure. Sir James Graham found it " tedious beyond endurance," and

Cockburn is even more severe: " This production, addressed as it is to all the prejudices of Toryism . . . is perhaps more inaccurate in its statements, worse reasoned, more absurd in its principles and views, and above all far worse written, than any other human composition." The pamphlet, however, did contain the main points in the case of the ultra-conservative intransigents.

CHAPTER V

THE ISSUES CLARIFIED

I

THE Auchterarder case had convinced the Non-Intrusionists that the spiritual independence of the Church was definitely in peril and that it was a matter of conscience to resist the aggression. Other cases had complicated the issue. At Lethendy, in Dunkeld Presbytery, a presentee was vetoed and appealed to the Court of Session, and later obtained an interdict to prevent the Presbytery from inducting another presentee. In this instance the Presbytery was of Evangelical persuasion, and following the instructions of the Commission of Assembly in August 1838, disobeyed the order of the civil courts to the extent of carrying through the admission, and for this they were reprimanded at the bar of the Court of Session. Later came the Culsalmond case and the Second and Third Auchterarder cases and others.

The case, however, which aroused most sentiment and most bitterness was that of the Banffshire parish of Marnoch in the Presbytery of Strathbogie. A vacancy being caused in 1837 by the death of William Stronach, a man of good social position who had been minister there for over thirty years, the presentation was given to John Edwards, schoolmaster in a neighbouring parish where his father had been the merchant. He was in his forty-fourth year, a worthy man with a turn for learning and a special interest in Hebrew ; but the appointment was an unfortunate one, for Edwards had been part-time assistant in the parish for several years during the decay of the incumbent, and according to the Evangelical paper, the *Aberdeen Banner*, " the parishioners were greatly dissatisfied with him, and on their representation he was removed from the office of assistant about a year before the minister died." A son of the late minister owned property in the district and was from the first "one of the most determined opponents of this settlement." There was a strong local desire that the appointment should go to David Henry, an Evangelical preacher who had succeeded Edwards as assistant and was carrying on the services during the vacancy. Local feeling was not friendly to Edwards, and some leading spirits found it easy to organize the parish against him, so that out of about 300 heads of families only one signed the "call," while 261 vetoed it. In accordance with instructions from the Assembly of 1838 the Presbytery rejected Edwards under the Veto Act, whereupon those responsible issued a presentation in favour of the people's candidate, Henry.

Edwards, regarding himself as a victim of personalities, fell back upon his rights under existing statute law ; and as the Auchterarder decision in the Court of Session (later confirmed by the House of Lords) declared that the Church had no competence to pass the Veto Act, that measure could not be recognized by the civil courts as of any authority, and an interdict was granted to stay proceedings at Marnoch. The Evangelical leaders wished the matter postponed till the Assembly of 1840, by which time they thought it possible that Government and Church might have come to some agreement on the general question ; and the Presbytery were therefore forbidden to travel further in the settlement. Edwards, however, obtained a decree of the civil court that as he had been legally presented the Presbytery were bound to proceed to the next step and take him on trials. The Presbytery were now in a very real difficulty. They were also divided in opinion. The majority, seven in number, were Moderates, respectable country ministers against whom personally no one had anything to object. The Seven relied in their later procedure upon the legal advice of John Hope.

They were now the representatives before the world of those who, in the light of recent political history at home and abroad, distrusted the democratic tendency behind the Veto Act, who feared that the cry of spiritual independence might produce nothing better than clerical tyranny without the useful check by public opinion which the State ought to provide, and

who were mindful of the Theocracy attempted by the Protesters
in the days of Cromwell. On constitutional grounds they
believed that it was a prime duty of citizens to obey the law :
if the law were found to be bad, one could hope to have it
altered ; but until then to disobey would be to give an evil
example of lawlessness to the serious detriment of society.   A
little patience might rectify any abuse ; and there was no need
for such sudden excitement about the intolerableness of
conditions which had prevailed for over a hundred years without
disaster, and under which the great majority of those now
agitating had been themselves ordained to the ministry.   They
were inclined to think the issue not one of principle but of
expediency.   So much for Law.   But there was also something
they could say on the side of Liberty, for did not their position
bear some resemblance to that of Ebenezer Erskine in 1733,
and to that of Thomas Gillespie in 1752, in insisting upon their
right to maintain a conscientious conviction even in opposition
to the highest court of the Church ?   Nor did they regard the
voice of a party that happened to be dominant as indeed the
voice of the Church.   They might have looked back to the
Glasgow Assembly of 1638 when a triumphant party acted
as the Church and meted out no gentle treatment to the
Episcopalian minority.   The House of Lords was the supreme
court of the land whose function it was to interpret the existing
law, and now that the law had been declared the Seven held it
to be their duty to obey, and that none the less because they
agreed with the decision as against the opinion of what happened
to be the majority in the Assembly.   What Dr Chalmers called
" the dance of that mazy and multiform confusion," or in less
characteristic but more popular language, " the Reel of Bogie,"
had begun.

There was an Evangelical minority of four ministers in
Strathbogie Presbytery, and they did their best to outmanœuvre
their brethren under the conviction that the proposed proceedings betrayed the rights of the people and were Erastian in
tendency, permitting State intervention in connection with the
spiritual acts of ordination and induction.   The minority were
supported by an almost entirely Evangelical Commission in

November 1839 ; but on 4th December, in spite of the Commission's explicit prohibition, but in accordance with the decision of the civil authorities, the majority decided to begin the trials of Mr Edwards. In order to prevent this the Commission a few days later suspended the Seven, declaring all ministerial acts which they might perform to be void and null. Mr Candlish made one of his most impassioned speeches, declaring that " intolerable offences have been committed against all ecclesiastical authority by our own ordained ministers," and that it was necessary to maintain the authority of the Church against " the encroachments of the civil arm," ' vindicating the supremacy of the General Assembly." Dr Chalmers also spoke " to defend our beloved Church from anarchy within and from that tyranny which now menaces and frowns upon us from without." An opposite view was upheld by Dr James Bryce, one of the extreme Moderates.

The suspension was confirmed by the Assembly of 1840. The Seven, however, disregarded the sentence, and in so doing they had the full support of the law courts which regarded the sentence as invalid, and also the support of the Moderate party who formed a league to uphold them, a measure which the Evangelicals answered by " engaging " in the opposite cause. They continued, therefore, to function as a court of the Church, meeting separately from the Four who, according to the dominant party, constituted the true Presbytery. Possibly, as John Cunningham the historian suggests, had they bowed to the ecclesiastical sentence, though holding that it amounted to persecution, little harm might have accrued to the cause they represented. The Commission, however, had decided to supply ordinances to the seven parishes, and this involved not simply that ministers were sent to Strathbogie to undertake the necessary duties, but that those selected for this work were naturally Evangelicals, and were consequently not mere substitutes but active agents of the rival party. To the Evangelicals it appeared that these parishes were now almost for the first time open to the Gospel. To the Moderates it appeared that the dominant party had taken advantage of its authority to plant officially in each of these parishes a missionary

F

of those narrow and fanatical influences which they had always conscientiously kept out. The Court of Session granted an interdict against the use by the intruders of the church premises ; and this was followed later by an " extended " interdict forbidding any minister to enter the parishes uninvited ; but even the extreme Moderates were not particularly easy about this latest intervention of the civil authorities, and though numerous representative Evangelicals conducted services and celebrated the sacraments within the seven parishes, none of the ministers entered formal complaint, and therefore the repeated breaches of interdict were not followed by any penalty. Tremendous local excitement was roused by the visiting preachers, and no doubt they would have welcomed arrest for the crime of breaking the interdict. We are told that Thomas Guthrie spoke in Strathbogie " with great fervour, and the feelings of the people were wrought to such a pitch that . . . he could have persuaded them to do almost anything, even to march up the valley, and pull down the old church and manse."

Mr Edwards now obtained a decision of the Court of Session that the Presbytery, having found him qualified, were according to the Acts of 1592 and 1712 bound to ordain and induct him ; and this they consequently proceeded to do. It is suggested that they might have sheltered behind their ecclesiastical suspension and declined responsibility ; but they chose to arrange the service for 21st January 1841, and Edwards was duly admitted. In the eyes of the protesting parishioners the Strathbogie Seven were suspended and contumacious clergy committing " the most daring act of intrusion ever perpetrated in this country." The scene at Marnoch has been frequently and fully described : the church on the hill which had been a religious centre long before Christianity was preached in the district, the ground covered with snow, an excited multitude of the curious and the sentimental from all the parishes round about, the crowded church, the proceedings resolutely transacted in spite of protest, the tense feeling and bitter indignation, the church members, profoundly touched, solemnly abandoning what had been the house of prayer but what they now believed had become a den of thieves, the mob ill-disposed and scarcely restrained from destructive rioting, the minister ordained and inducted but hissed at his own church door. Before long the congregation was collecting money from sympathizers all over the country, and a new church was erected and opened for worship in March 1842 with David Henry as minister, so that before the Disruption there were two ministers, two churches, two kirk sessions, and two congregations connected with the Church of Scotland within the parish. The situation resembled what occurred in some parts of the country in the schism between Resolutioners and Protesters in the days of the Covenant. There can be no doubt that people generally were shocked by the Marnoch induction.

But the drama was not yet over. It was not only in Strathbogie that excitement had reached fever-heat. The conduct of the Seven had become a central issue with the Evangelical leaders, and these ministers after a debate protracted to the early hours of morning were deposed by the Assembly of 1841. William Cunningham, speaking in support of the motion for deposition, declared that these men had broken the laws of the Church, had violated their ordination vows, and had been guilty of a sin against the Lord Jesus Christ. Dr Chalmers regarded their disobedience as " a blow struck at the entire jurisdiction of the Church." He was not impressed by their appeal to conscience, but opined " that if in heresy this plea were sustained the Church would be left without a creed ; and that if in contumacy this plea were sustained the Church would be left without a government ; both doctrine and discipline would be given to the winds." He held the dispute to be between the law courts and the Church, and appealed to the Legislature for adjustment. The Moderates, on the other hand, would have said rather that the dispute was between Church and State as contracting parties, with the law courts as the arbiter to interpret the arrangements and to judge as to their observance, the arrangements, if they proved unsatisfying, to be altered by negotiation. There was much argument, a great deal of it technical, but the essence of the charge against the Seven was that they had acknowledged the secular court to be supreme in matters spiritual over the judicatories of the Church.

Moderate leaders had not supported every act of the Seven, but in the debate their general position was strongly defended, and by none more ably than by James Robertson of Ellon. This rising leader, whom Hugh Miller was already calling " the redoubtable " and " the second name and first man of his party," possessed of " character, courage, momentum and unyielding firmness," the son of an Aberdeenshire farmer and a Bible-loving mother, was thrust through College at an early age and with the minimum of comfort, but did well in Mathematics, and became a most conscientious Divinity student. After some experience as a country schoolmaster, he was appointed Headmaster of Gordon's Hospital in Aberdeen, becoming minister at Ellon in 1832. He succeeded Dr Welsh as Professor of Church History at Edinburgh, and before his death in 1860 he had earned a special place in Scottish Church History by his devoted labours on behalf of the Endowment Scheme, which erected many new parishes to meet increasing population and so contributed substantially to the efficiency of the post-Disruption Church of Scotland. He retained a pronounced local accent, and his manner was brusque ; but when he spoke in the Assembly every word rang out clearly, and what he said, if it had perhaps a tendency to be exhaustive and over-analytic, was marked by evident sincerity, fairness, sagacity and clear thinking. His large-heartedness and his infectious enthusiasm gave him a strong and healthy influence.

The deposition of the Seven very seriously aggravated the situation, and public opinion which had disapproved of the Marnoch induction now disapproved of their treatment. It was felt that " they were just a concrete case of the general puzzle, and should be protected in the difficult position in which they found themselves till Church and State found a method of extricating all parties from what was recognised to be a matter of extreme complication." A Member of Parliament called them " victims of an atrocious tyranny " ; and public meetings attended by what the newspapers called " a numerous and highly respectable portion of the community," passed strongly worded motions of disapprobation of the action of the dominant party in the Church. The other side also had its crowded meetings, at one of which the chief speaker stirred his audience with these words : " To go into a parish and take away the religious instruction of two thousand people is terrible robbery, and if this were allowed we would soon become a nation of robbers and swindlers. It is a terrible thing to think that there should be seven men in the land who could be guilty of such profanity. Think of the mock prayer, of the mock sermon, of the mock ordination. . . . Here was an atrocious crime against men, an awful crime against God ; thousands sacrificed for the benefit of one. Was ever such profanity heard in Scotland ? It is enough to make the ears of any man tingle. Never was a fouler stain fixed on the annals of our history."

II

Marnoch may be said to have made the Disruption inevitable. The deposition created the final cleavage between the parties. The Moderates realized that their very existence was now in danger like that of the Bishops in 1638. It looked as if the next step would be an attempt to excommunicate them all. At a great meeting in Edinburgh, Candlish declared : " It is our bounden duty to bear this testimony that the Church ought to be established on the principles which we are contending for, or that there should be no establishment in the land at all " ; and referring to the Moderate minority, he said : " It is our bounden duty to use every effort that, if we be driven out, they shall be driven out too." And later he said : " We might tolerate a Voluntary Church, but we can never tolerate an Erastian one." And before the Assembly of 1842, Cunningham declared that steps must be taken to prevent Erastians entering the Ministry, the newspaper comment upon which was that all were to be excluded except such as were prepared to yield slavish obedience to the dominant party. After Marnoch, Dr Cook intimated that he proposed to raise the question as to whether the dominant party was the Church of Scotland, or whether the Legislature would not rather find those who obeyed the law to be entitled to the privileges and endowments conferred by statute on that Church. Meantime the Moderates declared that they could not recognize that the Seven were legally deposed, and they proceeded accordingly, for which later several of them were suspended.

The deposition had an unfortunate effect upon the politicians. The act seemed to be the sort of thing that should not be done during negotiations, and to be an obstinate flouting of the law of the land. It certainly became a definite obstacle in the way of a settlement through Government assistance.

The deposition had likewise an unhappy influence within the Evangelical party itself. There seems little doubt that the spirit of Candlish and others as revealed in this connection had considerable influence in creating those questionings and hesitations in the minds of many Evangelicals which presently led to the emergence of the Middle party, and eventually prevented these leaders from carrying with them when they went out that large and healthy group which later did so much for the preservation and resuscitation of the post-Disruption Church of Scotland.

From the political side several attempts were made to meet the ecclesiastical situation in Scotland. Interviews with Whig ministers in 1839 had made it clear that no official Government help need be expected. The Earl of Aberdeen, however, from the Tory side, offered his personal assistance, corresponded with the Non-intrusion leaders, and ultimately introduced a Bill into Parliament. The fourth Earl of Aberdeen, who was to become Prime Minister in 1852, was an earnest churchman, a zealous patriot, and a man of conscience, diligence and honesty. Gladstone wrote of him : " To my mind he has excelled every statesman now living in his sense of justice, his settled calm of mind, and the equipoise of his deliberative faculties." At first the Evangelical party viewed his intervention hopefully, but presently misunderstandings arose and eventually the Bill had to be withdrawn. The party certainly stiffened its claims as time passed and incidents occurred ; and Dr Chalmers, writing to Lord Aberdeen in 1840, says that he felt uneasy when he perceived " a tendency to rise in their demand." But the main cause of difference had reference to a point in the Veto

Act which the Evangelicals regarded as essential, and to the acceptance of which Lord Aberdeen found himself entirely opposed. The Veto Act expressly allowed for dissent without reasons. Mere dislike on the part of the parishioners was to be accepted as sufficient ground for the rejection of a presentee. The negotiating Non-intrusionists were willing that instead of a popular veto, there should be substituted power of veto by the Presbytery on objections stated by the people whether the reasons for these objections had any substance or relevancy ; but Lord Aberdeen would only go so far as to leave the matter entirely to the judgment of the Presbytery. Some persons might oppose a candidate because he had red hair. " This," said Lord Aberdeen, " would, no doubt, be a very bad reason ; but if they persevered in their hatred of red hair, and the Presbytery found it consistent with their sense of duty and the dictates of their own consciences, they might give effect to the objection by rejecting the presentee." This, however, was not enough for the Non-intrusionist leaders, who wished the final word to lie with the people, the Presbytery being empowered to reject on mere dislike expressed, which Lord Aberdeen felt amounted to a claim on the part of the Church to do exactly as it pleased with regard to any presentee and parish, and carried the doctrine of spiritual independence beyond proper limits. He formed the opinion that " there are some ' disturbed spirits ' whose element is agitation, and who, I much fear, do not greatly desire this settlement." Moderates felt that the Bill might have been accepted as at least very largely meeting the case, and that " the ruin of the Established Church of Scotland was far too heavy a price to pay for the difference between what it had been in their power to obtain and what it would have been agreeable, and perhaps even beneficial, to demand." Lord Aberdeen was annoyed at the turn of events, and later asserted in the House of Lords that " the presumption manifested by the General Assembly in these proceedings was never exceeded by the Church of Rome," a remark with which Lord Melbourne heartily agreed. Cunningham had so far departed from the proposals of Lord Aberdeen that he had characterized his Bill as " a great and grievous act of national sin tending to depose the Redeemer from His throne and to trample under foot the rights of His Church."

The next effort at a peaceful solution of the Scottish Church problem was by the Duke of Argyll, who introduced a measure which, to all intents and purposes, would have legalized the Veto Act of the Church, extending to all adult male communicants the right to dissent without stating reasons. The Bill had the support of the Assembly of 1841; but before the measure could be got through Parliament the political atmosphere changed and the Bill was shelved.

A third attempt was that of Sir George Sinclair, a well-meaning churchman, who succeeded in arranging a meeting between R. S. Candlish, the most determined and aggressive of the Non-intrusion protagonists, and John Hope, the legal mind behind many of the Moderate moves ; and the result was an effort to make Aberdeen's Bill more acceptable by introducing what came to be known as the *liberum arbitrium*, to the effect that a Presbytery might reject a presentee if it pleased, even if the objections stated did not impress the court, provided they were widely and strongly held, and provided also the Presbytery felt that they could not proceed with the settlement consistently with their duty and in the interests of the parish. According to this scheme it would not indeed be possible for the civil courts to interfere with a decision, but on the other hand there was nothing to prevent the Presbytery from intruding upon a congregation a man whom the majority did not wish to have. The Moderates did not like Sinclair's clause because it seemed to point in the direction of clerical despotism. The Government thought that if the law were to be changed at this stage the Strathbogie Seven who had suffered for obedience to the law as it formerly stood should be reponed or their deposition declared invalid. An ill-judged attempt by Sinclair and Hope to gain the submission of the Seven met with the natural rebuff. The Non-intrusionists, though at first satisfied, presently began to feel that allowance was scarcely made for mere aversion from a presentee being sufficient to ensure his rejection, and soon resiled from their support of the clause. One unfortunate result was that this brought to a head certain dissatisfaction that had been maturing within the party with regard to the extremer tone and attitude that now characterized the demands, and the Middle party emerged.

Sir George Sinclair, though friendly with everyone, had failed to please anyone ; but Campbell of Monzie, an Evangelical elder who had recently entered Parliament as member for Argyllshire, now proposed to revive the abandoned Bill of the Duke of Argyll. This Candlish and his party greatly preferred to Sinclair's more inadequate and meagre proposals ; and Campbell insisted to Government that his Bill was the only measure that could now prevent a Disruption. But the Government thought they could clear up the situation without yielding so much, and made it known that they were to bring in a Bill of their own. The reading of Campbell's Bill was first postponed, and then suddenly and conveniently the discovery was made that it was technically impossible to proceed with the Bill as it affected Crown rights.

There seems little doubt that it was the appearance of the Middle party that upset the attempt to have the Veto Act in all its completeness legalized. At a meeting of the Synod of Glasgow and Ayr a group of Evangelicals brought forward a Declaration that they were prepared to accept the Sinclair clause as they understood it, not as what they should like but as a fair compromise which would save the Church from the calamity of Disruption. It was indicated that forty members of the Synod had signed the Declaration, and the nickname of " the Forty " was soon improved by Hugh Miller to " the Forty Thieves," and clung to those in all parts of the country who, while sharing the ideals of the earlier Evangelicals, were unhappy about the feverish and excited zeal of Candlish which seemed to be driving the Church to Disruption. It appeared to them a matter of conscience and urgency even by sacrifice to preserve the unity of the Church rather than triumphantly to carry a point and vindicate an opinion at the price of schism. " The Forty " were for conciliation and accommodation. They did not regard the points of detail round which controversy now raged as more than non-essentials about which Christians could agree to differ ; and it was with dismay that they observed the unhallowed joy of the enemies of religion over the animosities that rent the Kirk.

The lead was taken by Matthew Leishman of Govan, handsome, scholarly, tolerant, with a high sense of the dignity of his office and a humble Christian faith, editor of Hugh Binning's *Works* and of Wodrow's *Analecta*, a faithful parish minister and an active promoter of Church extension. Other men of mark who associated themselves with him included Dr Simpson of Kirknewton, Presbytery and Assembly Clerk, the most prominent of the party ; Lockhart of Inchinnan, devout, cheerful, an assiduous pastor, a well-to-do laird, brother of Sir Walter Scott's son-in-law and biographer ; Robert Story of Rosneath, " a constitutional churchman . . . an evangelical theologian, and a most earnest and devoted minister " ; John Paul, the esteemed minister of St Cuthbert's, Edinburgh ; Lewis Balfour of Colinton, grandfather of Robert Louis Stevenson, who describes him in *Memories and Portraits* ; Nathaniel Morren of Greenock, and afterwards of Brechin, who has left us the valuable *Annals of the Church of Scotland, 1739-1766*, and who took an active part in the pamphlet warfare of the Ten Years' Conflict ; and Alexander Turner, who became minister of Port-of-Monteith and wrote *The Scottish Secession of 1843*, a judicial account of the Disruption movement. But the most interesting of those who joined this party was Norman Macleod, later of the Barony, Glasgow, one of the most robust of Christians, an unusual combination of initiative and broad-mindedness, endowed with energy, mental capacity, determination and sympathy, with an emotional Celtic nature, a lively sense of humour and a sincere interest in humanity, one who spoke always convincingly and from conviction. Gladstone called him " a great orator and pastor and a noble and true-hearted man." He took a busy interest in Foreign Missions and in practical social work, and edited the healthy religious periodical *Good Words* ; and his writings included the well-known *Starling* and *The Old Lieutenant and his Son*.

The Declaration was sent to the Government, who, being

badly served by those upon whom they depended for information as to the mind and will of Scotland, appear to have overestimated the possibilities of the new movement, and concluded that they might again hope for settlement along the lines suggested by Sinclair. But Candlish and his circle were very much upset by what he called " betraying the Church into the hands of her enemies." Sinclair's clause represented to him a barely possible minimum, and he had been hoping through Campbell of Monzie to have the full demands of his party conceded by Government. Now it seemed to those in authority as if all but a few intransigents would be well content with less. Leishman had written in his enthusiasm that he believed that " were the question settled upon the basis of Sir George's measure, according to his own explanation of it, it is questionable if a single minister would find himself driven to withdraw from the Church on the score of conscience." The Government felt that the situation was not after all so desperate, and that it was not urgent to yield to Campbell's demands. Buchanan gives an excellent summary of their impression : " A few hot-headed zealots might prefer to leap from the ramparts, and would, no doubt, as was confidently predicted, if not also charitably hoped, break their necks by the fall, but, as for the great bulk and body of the garrison there could be now no longer a doubt that they would by and by surrender at discretion." Candlish naturally felt that he had been wounded in the house of his friends ; and there was general denunciation of the " renegades." The well-known pamphlet *The Wheat and the Chaff* is a plain revelation of the extreme irritation caused to the Non-intrusionists by the Middle party.

III

The Assembly of May 1842 was one of the most eventful in Scottish Church History. Even the ceremonial procession according to a press account was arranged " on a scale of unprecedented splendour," " with all the concomitant circumstantialities." The *Witness* gives a vivid description of the scene : " The densely occupied galleries, with their 'overbellying crowds ' and where scarce an additional spectator could have found standing room, the fixity of posture, with the general movement at every pause, both so indicative of fixity of attention, the universal ' hush, hush,' when the slightest noise in some overcrowded corner threatened to rob the audience of but a fragment of the debate, the oneness of direction in every face, the forward attitude, the hand raised to the ear, all showed how thoroughly men are beginning to appreciate the importance of our great ecclesiastical struggle." Reviewing the proceedings afterwards, Hugh Miller remarks : " What a contrast from the days not long gone by, when a solitary amateur, Mr Creech the bookseller, was generally the only occupant of the gallery." The Assembly was meeting for the first time in St Andrew's Church, newly fitted up for their accommodation, and Miller notes " the uncompromising character of the majority " as they proceeded to business.

The repeated failures to produce a satisfactory modification of the existing Patronage system were bringing people to think that it might after all be as simple to abolish the obnoxious thing completely. In the 1842 Assembly even Dr Chalmers declared : " We have been shut up to this, that there is no conclusive and comfortable settlement but in the utter extinction of Patronage." A motion to this effect was at last on this occasion carried, and its opponents did not venture to word their countermotion more strongly than that it was " inexpedient in present circumstances to seek the abolition of Patronage." It was William Cunningham who had long led the anti-Patronage movement. He was to succeed Chalmers as Principal in 1847, and is described as tall and powerful in build, with a head " of the largest size, of the *nemo me impune lacessit* calibre," with a great shock of hair. He was no very inspiring teacher of Church History ; but in all the public controversies of those eventful years he took a full share. As a speaker he was logical, forceful, with a gift for sarcasm and a great command of information, a gladiator who gloried in conflict. At times, though he was of a generally mild and laconic temperament, he became very outspoken and had even to apologize for utterances made in the excitement of

enthusiastic meetings. Lord Cockburn thought him abler than
Candlish and a better speaker. Hugh Miller gives us further
light on his nature when he says : " White is always white with
Mr Cunningham, and black black, and he finds no shade of
grey in either."

By a large majority the Assembly agreed " that Patronage is
a grievance, has been attended with much injury to the cause
of true religion in this Church and Kingdom, is the main cause
of the difficulties in which the Church is at present involved,
and that it ought to be abolished." Cunningham was right in
claiming that the passing of this resolution " constituted an
era in the history of the Church of Scotland." An Address on
the subject was at once transmitted to Government, along
with the *Claim of Right* of the same Assembly. The answer
over the signature of Sir James Graham was long in coming ;
but its argument plainly turned more upon the anti-Patronage
demand than upon anything in the other document. There
was not at the moment the remotest chance that the British
Parliament would immediately consent to the abolition of
Patronage in Scotland, however willing it might be to talk about
reforming the existing ecclesiastical arrangements ; and the
reply expressed the conviction that the Church of Scotland
under Patronage had fulfilled its purposes well, and " any
shock which might endanger this great national establishment
would be regarded by Her Majesty's servants as a fearful
calamity." The *Claim of Right* was unfortunately read in the
light of the anti-Patronage Address, and the reply concluded
with the statement : " Her Majesty's ministers now understanding that nothing less than the total abrogation of the
rights of the Crown and of other patrons will satisfy the Church,
are bound with firmness to declare that they cannot advise Her
Majesty to consent to the grant of any such demand." Sir
James Graham was a reasonable person and a religious man,
but he had come to the conclusion that the dominant party in
the Church wanted everything into their own hands and had
no respect for the law, and that to legislate on the suggested
lines for such people would be absurd.

The Assembly of 1842 produced also that most important

of the documents in the case, the *Claim of Right*. This was put forward after very careful preparation by Alexander Murray Dunlop, who has consequently been described as the " modern Warriston " responsible for this " modern Solemn League and Covenant," an acute and discerning lawyer, descended from William Carstares and from the Dunlop who edited the valuable *Collection of Confessions of Faith*, a most devoted young churchman, entirely disinterested ; in Lord Cockburn's phrase, " the purest of enthusiasts," and in Thomas Guthrie's words, " a man of such delicate honour, so incapable by nature as well as grace of anything low or mean, and withal a devout, humble Christian."

The *Claim of Right* is a long document, for the most part minutely historical but concluding with four paragraphs which were afterwards regarded as practically the constitution of the Free Church. Christ was declared to be the only Head of the Church, and to have appointed church officers to govern in spiritual matters and to have the power of the keys. The State had its own functions associated with the power of the sword. The exclusive jurisdiction of the Church within its own province was confirmed by a succession of Acts of Parliament, and the sense in which these were to be interpreted was indicated from time to time in connection with critical historical incidents. Civil rights and privileges were secured to the Church and its courts by various statutes, one of which expressly described " intrusion " as " an high contempt of the law," and similarly condemned the performance of any act of ecclesiastical duty by a minister deposed. In 1707 a fundamental condition of the Treaty of Union between England and Scotland was that the Protestant religion and the worship, discipline and government of the Church of Scotland should not be altered at any time thereafter. The law and practice as to Patronage and the call were stated. Allusions were made to the Auchterarder judgment by which the Veto Act was declared illegal. Then followed references to instances in which the courts were alleged to have " refused to interfere with the peculiar functions and exclusive jurisdiction of the courts of the Church." Thereafter came a list of examples to illustrate the invasion of the jurisdiction of the Church and encroachments upon its spiritual privileges, " in violation of the constitution of the country, in defiance of the statutes above-mentioned, and in contempt of the laws of this kingdom," and the Court of Session was stated to have usurped the power of the keys. The Church's State connection was alluded to with appreciation, while the claim was advanced that the Church " shall freely possess and enjoy her liberties, government, discipline, rights, and privileges, according to law, especially for the defence of the spiritual liberties of her people." It was declared that the Church must refuse to intrude ministers on reclaiming congregations even at the risk of losing the public advantages of an establishment, and the document went on to protest that acts of Parliament or decisions of Courts in any contrary sense would be regarded as void and null. Finally a summons was made on Christian people in Scotland and Christian Churches elsewhere holding the doctrine of the sole Headship of Christ to witness that it was for adherence to that doctrine that the Church of Scotland was now in peril.

The Evangelical party accepted this remarkable document with acclamation. Dr Buchanan says of it : " Its style grave and perspicuous, its tone calm and solemn, its facts well chosen, accurately stated and lucidly arranged, its argument direct and powerful, its conclusion clear and resolute, it must ever be regarded by all intelligent and candid readers as every way worthy of the great occasion on which it was to be employed." In the Assembly the Claim, Declaration and Protest was eloquently supported by Dr Chalmers ; and Dr Gordon of the High Church, calm, dignified and resolute, in seconding, declared : " We cannot carry on the affairs of Christ's house under the coercion of the civil courts ; and however deeply we may deplore the loss of those advantages which we derive from our connection with the State, if ultimately the Legislature determine that they will not listen to our claim, then those advantages we must relinquish, because we could not hold them with a good conscience."

The Moderate party reply put forward by Dr Cook took the form of resolutions to the effect that the Veto Act, having been pronounced illegal, should be abandoned ; that there is room for conscientious diversity of opinion as to the application of the principles of the Headship of Christ and Spiritual Independence, as to the line of demarcation between the provinces of Church and State, and as to what constitutes intrusion ; that the situation does not justify schism and the present agitation should therefore cease and the Church return to its normal work ; and that there is in fact " great security against the settlement of unqualified and unjustifiable ministers, whilst ample opportunities are afforded to the office-bearers of the Church as members of the different ecclesiastical judicatories to propose in a legal and constitutional manner any measures which may appear to them calculated to increase that security."

The narrative part of the *Claim of Right* is strongly coloured by party opinion, and does justice only to one line of conviction within the Church of Scotland throughout its history. It is in fact a manifesto, and the interpretations made and the references drawn are plainly not the only possible interpretations and inferences. A Moderate pamphleteer was able to produce what appeared to him satisfactory evidence that there was in the *Claim of Right* a great amount of historical misrepresentation ; and when it is baldly stated, for example, that the Court of Session held ministers " liable in damages for refusing to break their ordination vows " we have what is clearly not a simple record of fact, but a judgment based upon personal views as to the ultimate implications of the Court's decision. But the massing of the information in the first part and the powerful statement of claim, declaration, protest and summons at the close constituted an extremely useful document for crystallizing and confirming Evangelical opinion and heightening feeling at a critical moment.

The *Claim of Right* was sent along with the Address on the Abolition of Patronage to the Government, who not unnaturally viewed them together and in the light of a further *Memorial* to Sir Robert Peel, which was transmitted in December 1842 ; and the letter signed by Sir James Graham on 4th January 1843 was intended as the official reply to all three. The *Memorial* had stated that the Church was " entitled to know whether the

Government of the country are to rest upon the views of the constitution of the Church now acted upon by the courts of law, or are willing to adopt measures for securing her in the possession of those privileges which she considers to belong to her under that constitution." It also declared plainly that by certain of the legal decisions of which complaint was made, ' the constitution of the country has been broken, and that vested rights and privileges secured by statute and solemn national treaty have been violated." The reply traces the trouble to the Veto Act of 1834, " an attack on vested rights secured by statute," and says that the doctrine of Spiritual Independence as the Church understands it appears to imply not only irresponsible authority but that the Church is to be sole judge as to what matters are spiritual. When spiritual and civil powers co-exist it is difficult to define the precise limit of their spheres. The Church has been apt to feel that in resisting the civil authorities it is suffering for conscience' sake ; but its pretensions have had to be resisted in the interest of civil liberty, and when it is not evident within whose jurisdiction a particular matter falls, the problem is one for the law courts. The claim put forward by the Church would mean despotic power ; but the Veto Act was passed upon this illegal assumption that the Church's legislative and judicial proceedings are beyond the cognizance of the courts. The letter reminds the Church leaders of the maxim of the *Second Book of Discipline*, that the Church should not meddle with anything pertaining to the civil jurisdiction, a doctrine confirmed by the *Westminster Confession*. A patron's right belongs to the civil jurisdiction, and in passing the Veto Act the Assembly intermeddled with civil affairs. The Auchterarder judgments were plain, and subsequent cases had been applications of these legal decisions. There had been hopes of amendment of the position along the lines of Lord Aberdeen's Bill to remove doubts as to the respective rights of the patron to present, the Congregation to object, and the Church courts to admit or reject ; but the Non-intrusionists' demands were not such as Government could grant.

G

IV

Before this Letter was received there had been taken one
of the most dramatic and effective steps in the procedure of the
Evangelicals in the summoning of the Convocation of November
1842.   For such as still hoped for settlement it was important
to demonstrate to Government and all concerned the extent
of the party following and the reality of the party threat to
abandon the Establishment.   For such as held separation to be
now inevitable it was vital to make sure that the ministers
whose temporal future would be critically affected by a Disruption were prepared to face the possibilities and committed to
common action.

The organization of the party was already highly developed.
The best propaganda methods had been continuously employed.
The men who directed the movement were intelligent, zealous
and determined, and possessed of a shrewd understanding of
human nature.   Meetings in all parts of the country had been
arranged, and crowded audiences addressed with debating skill
and moving sentiment by convinced and ardent speakers.   The
Witness, edited with genius by Hugh Miller, was the party
guide on doctrine and fact, and like the newspapers on the other
side used all the known weapons of attack and all the known
methods of defence.   Exhaustive and acrimonious discussions
took place at successive Presbytery meetings.   Feeling throughout the country became increasingly bitter.   The time had
passed when reconciliation by Act of Parliament could be
regarded as likely.   In the circumstances the summoning of
the Convocation was a piece of ecclesiastical statesmanship,
and for this Chalmers was largely responsible.   The meeting
was private, for ministers only, and only for ministers who
were understood to be of evangelical persuasion.   Hospitality
in Edinburgh was provided and a fund was raised to meet
travelling expenses.   Even the absence of the minister from
his parish and pulpit was used to impress upon the people
the seriousness of the situation.   Elders were encouraged to
hold prayer-meetings in connection with the congregations
during the critical week ;   attention was called to relevant

Bible passages, and all concerned were exhorted to penitence, faithfulness, wisdom and harmony.

The gathering was held in the Roxburgh Church. It was well handled, and although inevitably some difference of opinion and some temper revealed themselves, the result was very much to the satisfaction of the organizers. The Convocation was meant to be a conference rather than a succession of speeches by leaders, and devotional exercises were a solemnizing feature of the proceedings. High ideals as to duty and sacrifice were set forth, and there was much evidence of deep conviction. Some were led to give their concurrence to the decisions because impressed by the belief that a strong stand now would render secession unnecessary ; some who hesitated from considerations of prudence were caught by the general enthusiasm ; some were reassured by the cheering financial prospects which Dr Chalmers, whose success in money-raising was proverbial, expounded with such optimism that (as one speaker hinted) the life-boat was made to look better than the ship.

A sympathetic contemporary account thus describes the event : " The fathers and brethren of the Church of Scotland met in Convocation, including all among her teachers whose labours have been most eminently blessed by God, all who are most endeared to her people, all that are most venerable and venerated for purity of character and depth of piety, have solemnly determined, trusting in the divine help, that they shall be the ministers of a free Church of Christ and of a free Church only." The text of the opening sermon by Dr Chalmers in St George's showed the same assured spirit: " Unto the upright there ariseth light in the darkness " ; and his inspiration was noticeable throughout the Convocation.

Among the chief orators was Dr Robert S. Candlish, minister of St George's, Edinburgh, who since his first speech in the Assembly of 1839 had become, though not so much in the public eye as Chalmers, the real leader of the party. He was still under forty, small and slim, but with a great forehead, a preacher eccentric in manner but of notable intellect, fervour and power, a clear and ready and vigorous speaker, a clever and persuasive debater, gifted with some originality and versatility and a talent for clarifying issues, a theologian of metaphysical subtlety but strictly Calvinistic orthodoxy, in private life simple and tender, sensitive, but above all, unselfish. None of the Disruption Fathers was so much disliked by the Moderates, who thought him an unscrupulous intriguer. At the time of his death in 1861 he was Principal of New College, Edinburgh. According to Dr Candlish the Convocation bore testimony to the duty of the Church to acknowledge the authority of Christ and that alone, and the duty of the civil magistrate to acknowledge Christ and to protect Christ's servants. " Both Church and State," he said, " are bound to acknowledge Christ and Christ alone. Each has its sphere, but therein each must serve Christ." Fears that the party were drifting towards Voluntaryism were allayed by his avowal : " Never at any time have the intelligent ministers and elders and friends of the Church been in less danger of becoming Voluntaries than they are at this moment."

The position of the Evangelicals was stated thus by Cunningham : " If the Legislature, whose prerogative alone it was to determine the conditions upon which the Church was to enjoy a State endowment, should either reject or disregard the final appeal of the Church for the establishment of her inherent rights as a Church of Christ, they must renounce their connection with the State, and thus forfeit the benefits of an established Church rather than the character of a Church of Christ."

Two sets of Resolutions were put to the gathering. The first, a statement of principles, included propositions to the effect that according to the law courts the obligation to admit a qualified presentee is a civil obligation, and his rejection on account of the dissent of a congregation is a civil offence ; that other legal decisions assume that the courts have jurisdiction in ecclesiastical matters such as the deposing of ministers ; that such claims are based on the Act of 1712 to which as now interpreted the Church can no longer submit ; that the principle involved in these decisions is that of the supremacy of the civil courts over those of the Church of Scotland in the exercise of their spiritual functions and against such encroachments the Church must be protected ; and that the present tendencies are subversive of the constitution of the country. This group received the adherence of 423 of the ministers present.

The second set dealt with the remedy, and included protests against the invasion of the Church's jurisdiction by the civil courts as contrary to the Treaty of Union of 1707, declaring that refusal by the State to remedy the situation will amount to an acceptance by the State of the principle involved in the law decisions ; that the Church recognizes the right of the State to fix the terms on which it will grant an establishment ; that ministers should not accept endowments on the condition of subjection to civil control in spiritual matters ; and that the Church should make plain its recognition of the benefits of an establishment, but also the perils in which the establishment now stands and the possibility of disruption and of resignation from the civil advantages which can no longer be held in consistency with the free and full exercise of spiritual functions, the ministers casting themselves on such provision as God may afford, while maintaining the principle of an establishment. Those who adhered to these resolutions numbered 354.

CHAPTER VI
THE PARTING OF THE WAYS

I

THE Convocation resolutions amounted to a pledge of separation unless Government yielded to the demands of the *Claim of Right*. There can be no doubt that these meetings gave the party cohesion, confirmed weaker brethren, and strengthened the confidence of the leaders in their plans. Many of the ministers on returning to their parishes held special gatherings to report and to encourage adherence to the proposed scheme for separation. The Session of an Edinburgh church pledged itself to go out if Parliament proved obdurate, and declared that " a church of Christ cannot faithfully perform the duties which it owes to its divine Head unless it is permitted to exercise full, free, exclusive and supreme jurisdiction in all matters spiritual, in which we include the fixing the qualifications and conditions essential to the foundation of the pastoral relation." A meeting of sympathetic elders in the capital adhered to the Resolutions of the Convocation. Public opinion was stimulated by an *Address to the People of Scotland* emphasizing the dangers that threatened " the inherent liberty " of the Church, and claiming communion with those who had endured persecution for conscience' sake since the Reformation, including " the poor peasantry of Scotland " who suffered in the days of the Covenants. The attention of Government was also called to the convictions and determinations of those attending the Convocation by a *Memorial* to Peel, containing the Resolutions and pointing out " the inevitable result of a continued refusal on the part of the Legislature of that indispensable measure of relief which they think they have a good reason to ask and good reason to expect." The party could not remain in the communion of a Church that agreed " to regulate her procedure according to the principles now held to be involved in the civil law."

W. G. Blaikie, speaking of the period after the Convocation, says : " We had all now to busy ourselves with preparation for the Disruption." Guthrie writes of the great work done by Hugh Miller in the *Witness* and by those who did deputation duty through the country ; but for this education for the Disruption, it would have been, he says, " a great failure." Dr Chalmers at the Convocation had said : " Organize, organize, organize." Dr Beith, who took part in the work, prefers O'Connell's word " Agitate," and his account of his efforts he calls " my narrative of agitation." A central committee in Edinburgh with auxiliary associations in a multitude of places was busy making plans and raising money and arranging meetings. The deputies were often blamed for the way in which they broke the quiet of peaceful parishes by their exciting story of crisis and their call to secede. Proprietors were also blamed for making difficulties about churches or halls for these gatherings, while themselves propagating at other meetings a different tale of " the audacious attempt to encroach upon the rights of liberty and property which has been evinced by this ecclesiastical faction." The feelings of the rural population on the Evangelical side may be sampled in such a classic as *Johnny Gibb of Gushetneuk* ; and a different point of view is expressed in Norman Macleod's *Cracks aboot the Kirk for Kintra Folk.* There was an amazing quantity of pamphlets on the market for all types of readers.

The Assembly of 1834 which passed the Veto Act had enacted another measure of importance—the Chapel Act. The splendid Church Extension movement which Dr Chalmers had served so devotedly had helped to bring into existence a large group of churches supernumerary to the old parish churches and often serving busy sections of such parishes. Those who connected themselves with these churches included the pioneers of the new industries and the new residential areas in the larger towns, keen people whose zeal made them active church members. Many of the ministers who were prepared to undertake the building up of these new congregations and who were selected and paid by their congregations were of the most consecrated type. There was useful work being done, and these congregations were as enthusiastic as the most earnest Evangelical could wish. All such new charges suffered, however, under serious disadvantages. The old parish system was very inelastic, and the new churches had only chapel status and had no kirk-session of their own, while the minister had no right to a seat in Presbytery, Synod or Assembly, and no territory was officially assigned him as a parish. It was unfortunately only with the greatest difficulty that under the existing law a new parish in the fullest sense of that word could be delimited and endowed with teind stipend and all privileges. There was something quite un-Presbyterian about this chapel idea. It was out of accord with the principle of parity of clergy about which a great deal of fuss had at times been made in Scotland. There was also an obvious inferiority in the position and opportunity of the minister and congregation when compared with what prevailed in Voluntary denominations. The Church of Scotland chapels were handicapped.

It was clear that something ought to be done to remedy the anomaly, and a Declaratory Act in 1833 was followed next year by the Chapel Act. Dr Chalmers and some other Evangelicals hesitated before this proposal, being very much afraid of encouraging Voluntaryism within the Church of Scotland. It had, however, eloquent support from chapel ministers, who advocated the scheme from the bar of the Assembly, and on the motion of Professor R. J. Brown of Marischal College, Aberdeen, was carried against a counter-proposal by Dr Cook to approach Government with a view to the erection of these charges into parishes and also to make plans for their endowment. The Moderates were not very favourably inclined to the chapels, which they looked on as cells of dissent inside the Church of Scotland.

The Act facilitated Church Extension. Before the Disruption some 200 chapels had been granted full status as parish churches *quoad sacra* and their ministers given full rights on Church courts. The Act also opened a way by which dissenting congregations might return to the fold of the Church of Scotland ; and in 1839 most of the Old Light Burgher ministers and people, including Thomas McCrie, the popular biographer of Knox and Melville, unobtrusively resumed their place within the old Church. An Old Light Burgher congregation in Stewarton, a village in the Ayrshire Presbytery of Irvine, was thus received ; but the proposal to delimit a parish and to add the minister's name to the Presbytery roll called forth an interdict from heritors to prevent " innovating upon the present parochial state of the parish of Stewarton as regards pastoral superintendence, its kirk-session, jurisdiction and discipline." A Court of Session case developed, and in January 1843 the judges, by a majority of eight to five, declared the Chapel Act illegal. It was again the problem of the relation of Church and State, the problem of Spiritual Independence, the problem of the delimitation of spheres. To the Evangelical party the decision amounted to a ruling that the civil courts had " the power to prevent the Church of Scotland from extending the means of spiritual instruction to the community as necessity required," to which they felt convinced the Church " could not submit without ceasing to be a Church of Christ." To the Moderate party it rather appeared that the existence of vested rights relating to the territorial arrangements and to the membership of Church courts had been confirmed ; and that the Church was not the competent body to legislate on such matters, there being in existence machinery for erecting new parishes and for modifying the membership of Church courts, which machinery the authorities could be pressed to render more effective than it admittedly had been.

The judgment of the Court, though expected, came at an awkward time. The Non-intrusionists were preparing for the inevitable Disruption in May ; but now doubt was cast upon the validity of all decisions made since 1834 by Church courts which included chapel ministers, and all chapel ministers were disqualified from voting in Presbytery, Synod or Assembly, which was a matter of great importance, as the Evangelical strength was immediately and seriously reduced in many Presbyteries and the party balance altered. The representatives to the ensuing vital General Assembly would now, if the validity of the decision were admitted, have to be elected by bodies from which these numerous Evangelical chapel ministers would be excluded, and they could not themselves be elected to attend the Assembly, where in consequence the party would certainly not have the majority to which it had become accustomed. What confusion ensued may be illustrated from the fact that the Presbytery of Irvine split into two rival courts : one consisting of those who accepted the decision of the law court and refused to recognize chapel ministers as any longer members of Presbytery, the other of those who insisted on retaining the chapel ministers with them to form the Presbytery. At the Assembly in May there were present in some cases two sets of representatives from such rival Presbyteries ; and possibly the decision to leave for the Tanfield Hall before the Assembly was constituted was influenced by the fact that it could not now be established that a legal majority of the Assembly were prepared to separate. Had the Stewarton decision been different it might have been practicable to constitute the Assembly and then officially renounce the State connection, which would indeed have been the Disruption of the Church from the State as Chalmers envisaged it.

As a last effort in the direction of settlement, Mr Fox Maule presented to Parliament in February 1843 a petition from the Special Commission of Assembly which had considered the position created by the Government's explicit refusal through Sir James Graham to grant the demands of the *Claim of Right*. He was supported by Andrew Rutherford, who had been Counsel for the defenders in the Auchterarder case. Lord Campbell raised the matter in the House of Lords. The Government, however, had made up its mind, and nothing could be achieved against its opposition. In spite of the Convocation the Ministers of the Crown, misled by Lord Dunfermline and others who misjudged the situation in Scotland, did not believe that a serious secession was in the least likely.

II

On 18th May 1843 met the Disruption Assembly of the Church of Scotland. The heavy responsibility of guiding at the beginning this representative gathering of ministers and elders on this momentous occasion fell to Dr David Welsh, Professor of Ecclesiastical History at Edinburgh, a talented Evangelical, at that date still in middle life. He has been described as thin, pale and somewhat delicate, well-liked for his open heart and pleasant manner, and highly respected for his acute mind and balanced judgment. Cockburn says he was " perfectly free from fanaticism and illiberality ; amiable, well-bred, temperate, learned and quietly able." Welsh had reached his chair and the Moderatorship at an early age partly on the reputation he made by his biography of his master, Dr Thomas Brown.

Welsh was present with other leaders at the preliminary party meeting in St Luke's Church on the Monday, Tuesday and Wednesday ; and then came the service in St Giles', when he preached from the appropriate text : " Let every man be fully persuaded in his own mind." Beith pictures him in the pulpit before the service began " rolling his tongue about in his mouth, according to his usual habit, as if he were chewing it." He was not very well, and read his sermon with somewhat staccato enunciation and in a voice not easily audible. It was not an eloquent sermon, but informative, sensible and solemnizing. Norman Macleod thought it the beau-ideal.

The Assembly then met in St Andrew's Church, George Street, the ecclesiastical parties sitting separately as they had unhappily learned to do, the Moderates on the right and the Evangelicals on the left of the Commissioner's throne and the Moderator's chair, while an excited public filled the galleries. All stood as the Moderator entered in his robes and lace, and the customary formal bows were exchanged with both sides of the house. The Queen's Commissioner, the Marquis of Bute, appeared with his suite. Prayer followed, but the roll was not made up and the Assembly was not constituted. Instead, the Moderator read a carefully worded *Protest*, subscribed by over 200 of the Evangelicals present, declaring that in existing circumstances a free Assembly of the Church of Scotland, " in accordance with the laws and constitution of the said Church," was impossible, since the Legislature had rejected the *Claim of Right* and refused protection against the civil courts which were claiming authority in matters spiritual. The signatories complained that "they are subject to be compelled to intrude ministers on reclaiming congregations in opposition to the fundamental principles of the Church"; and that civil courts have power to interdict the preaching of the Gospel as authorized by Church courts, to suspend spiritual censures pronounced by Church courts, and to determine as to the right of membership in Church courts. It was further complained that because of the decision against the Chapel Act, certain representatives elected to that Assembly were liable to be interdicted from claiming their seats. The document went on to state that such were evidently the conditions under which the Establishment was now to be permitted, and that, as the signatories were not prepared to accept these conditions, they could not in conscience continue connected with and retain the benefits of that Establishment. They protested that the conditions of which they complained were subversive of the Revolution Settlement, and incompatible with the freedom essential to the Church and the Government which Christ as Head of the Church had appointed distinct from the civil magistrate. It was maintained that the *Claim of Right* set forth the true constitution of the Church of Scotland, and a concluding reference was made to " this our enforced separation from the Establishment which we loved and prized, through interference with conscience, the dishonour done Christ's crown, and the rejection of his sole and supreme authority as King in His Church."

It was possible for the *Protest* to be thus read because the presiding Moderator happened to be a member of the protesting party. When the reading was finished, Dr Welsh laid the document on the table and moved according to plan to the door on his left, and he was followed from the building by those on the front Evangelical bench—Dr Chalmers, Dr Gordon, Dr Patrick McFarlan, Dr Candlish and Dr Cunningham. Quietly, and in order, pew by pew, ministers and elders stepped out, and marched in procession, according to Beith, " three abreast, arm in arm," along George Street and down Hanover Street to Tanfield. The event was expected ; the city was all excitement ; the populace and the many friends of the Assembly members from all over the country were lining the street and voiced the liveliest interest and sympathy and satisfaction. Seldom in Scottish history has any scene aroused such emotion. Alexander Dunlop had visited the Tanfield Hall some time previously, and describes it thus : " It was used as a wareroom ; and on its extensive floor, otherwise vacant, stood here and there piles of boxes of oranges. The day was snowy, and the stone floor and dreary void gave it an aspect of coldness and deadness, the recollection of which now forms a strong contrast to the spectacle often afterwards seen there, of the solemn assembly of those who had witnessed a good confession for Christ, sur- rounded by tier upon tier of an earnest audience, all animated with a warm and holy enthusiasm, and engaged in doings of which the memory will never die." In due course the company were gathered in this large hall, furnished for the occasion. The place was crowded, and the prevailing spirit was solemn but exultant.

Professor Welsh took the chair, and this involved a claim, often repeated, that the gathering was still the Assembly of the Church of Scotland, though now free from the State connection, that in fact the Disruption was that of the Church from the State. Dr Chalmers was by acclamation elected Moderator, and the renown and popularity of the man who was now formally, as he had long been actually, in the forefront of the movement, played a part in colouring the impression which these events made upon the country at large and upon Churches elsewhere.

III

" There were," declared Henry Cockburn, " four men who, in my time, have made Scotland illustrious—Dugald Stewart, Walter Scott, Thomas Chalmers, and Francis Jeffrey." Thomas Chalmers, born in 1780 at Anstruther in Fife, was a merchant's son, and from being a healthy and none too studious schoolboy, awakened as a student at St Andrews University to a passion for Mathematics and Science, drifted into the ministry, and

settled in the parish of Kilmany so close to his old college that
he was able to spend much of his week teaching his favourite
subjects ; but in so doing, as he afterwards admitted, he overlooked two magnitudes, the littleness of time and the greatness
of eternity. Religion presently came to new power and place
in his life : he began to take a deeper interest in theology ;
and he became a zealous pastor and, though he never lost his
broad Scots pronunciation and provincial accent, a pulpit orator
unusually stirring and effective. He was minister of the Tron
Kirk in Glasgow from 1815 to 1819, and in this period his
popularity as a preacher was phenomenal, and when he delivered
a series of sermons in London, his crowded and enthusiastic
audiences included leaders in the political world, the Church,
literature and fashionable society. We are told of " the breath-
lessness of expectation," the Prime Minister affected even to
tears, Wilberforce reporting " all the world wild about
Dr Chalmers." Then came the experiment at St John's,
Glasgow, where Chalmers the practical organizer revealed
himself in the attempt to vindicate the endowed territorial
system in the city, and the ability of the kirk-session through
voluntary church collections to provide for poor relief adequately
and with the best moral and spiritual results. He was heartily
in line with the Scottish Reformers, who assigned to minister
and session the spiritual supervision of an area, and included
in their responsibilities the care of the young and of the poor.
Ignorance and poverty he believed to be the enemies of a well-
ordered community. He was worried about the condition of
the people, and was convinced that nothing but religious
influence would save the situation. The National Church had
a duty to the whole population and was capable under proper
guidance of performing this duty. There was indeed no attempt
on his part at the prevention of the evils that had come to be
associated with the industrial advance of the country ; but he
aimed at making effective in the new circumstances the ameliora-
tive work which the Church had always conventionally professed
to do. His experiment was up to a point remarkably successful,
though it did not permanently affect the social problem.

Some years at St Andrews as Professor of Moral Philosophy

helped to prepare Chalmers for the Divinity Chair in Edinburgh, which he occupied from 1828 until 1843, when he became the first Principal of the Free Church College in that city, a position which he retained till his sudden death in 1847. He wrote on Ethics, Economics, Dogmatics and Apologetics ; but he had a contented scholastic mind and showed no creative faculty in dealing with the problems of these sciences, nor was he in very close touch with advanced contemporary thought in any province, which is no doubt what Thomas Carlyle had in mind when he referred to the " narrow sphere " in which all Chalmers's activities took place. At the same time he was the most potent spiritual influence in Scotland for a generation. Portraits and descriptions reveal a square-built figure, somewhat heavy features, pale, with lack-lustre eyes which, however, lighted up marvellously in moments of excitement, careless locks of strong dark hair, fading to silver in later years, a noble forehead, an expressive mouth, and a firm jaw. " Everybody," says Cockburn, " loved the quaint, picturesque oddity of his look, figure and manner ; his self-coined diction and thick articulation ; his taste for cumbrous jokes and the merry twinkle of the eye." In character he was benevolent and genial, guileless and unsophisticated, of devout religious habits, conscientious and energetic but not fussy, imperious but not arrogant, capable of intense concentration and of burning enthusiasm. Intellectually solid but not outstanding, he impressed much more by his personality than by learning or originality, and made his conquests by capture rather than by negotiation. He was himself susceptible to prevailing views and easily influenced by strong-willed associates, and thus was rather the champion than the director of the Disruption movement ; but he always remained both a doughty upholder of the national establishment and a hearty believer in spiritual independence. One of his most celebrated utterances was that in which he touched upon the latter subject in a lecture in London upon the former.

There can be no doubt as to his genius in oratory and in organizing. The general opinion about his pulpit work was that of Lockhart : " Most unquestionably I have never heard, either in England or Scotland or in any other country, any preacher whose eloquence is capable of producing an effect so strong and so irresistible as his." Jeffrey on one occasion expressed the conviction that " never had eloquence produced a greater effect upon a popular assembly." His style was marked by grandiloquence, a fondness for long and curious words, for alliteration, for duplicating verbs or adjectives, for balancing clauses ; but there is an overwhelming fluency and there are highly imaginative illustrations and many pregnant phrases. When his sermons were first published, Hazlitt tells how they " ran like wildfire through the country ; were the darlings of watering-places, were laid in the windows of inns, and were to be met with in all places of public resort." The modern reader wearies of the frequent redundancies and the constant and almost maddening repetitions, and there is a lack of literary and historical allusion ; but the hearer was completely carried away by rolling periods, effective rhetorical questions, successions of short telling sentences, and, gilded with his passionate locution, even commonplace thought seemed interesting and important. An excellent description is from James Dodds : " No more constraint now, no more awkwardness, no more feebleness of voice and manner : he has the mastery of his subject, he has the mastery of his audience. The voice, without sweetness or melody indeed, has the thrill of the clarion, summoning to battle for the right and against all wrong and evil. The eye, which was dull and half-closed is all on fire with intelligence and rapture and zeal . . . the breast heaves with the tumult of only half-uttered thoughts, the strong arm is uplifted in rebuke, or spread out with proffers of mercy. . . . Reasoning, illustration, appeal, with swift successive strokes, carry captive every mind." Chalmers was never a ready speaker, and closely read his sermons and speeches ; but this did not seem to obstruct the overpowering earnestness and intensity of his eloquence. As for his adversaries in debate, Jeffrey said that he buried them " under fragments of burning mountains."

A remarkably expert organizer he was besides, and contributed to the Disruption as much by administrative planning of details as by floods of oratory. His genius had been displayed in the scheme which he elaborated for the spiritual and social work in St John's, and later in the astonishing success of his efforts to raise money for Church Extension. It is true that his Glasgow plan was superseded, and his scheme for State Endowment fell through on account of Voluntary opposition ; true also that he seemed to vacillate, not being sure at first about the Veto Bill, not sure about the Chapel Act, not wholly against Patronage nor wholly for popular election, not certain what steps to take after the Auchterarder case ; but when his course was decided his enthusiasm and consecration were invaluable, and in no effort more effective than in what he achieved for the Free Church in originating and organizing its secure and stable Sustentation Fund. Said Thomas Carlyle : " It is not often that the world has seen men like Thomas Chalmers, nor can the world afford to forget them. . . . Honour belongs to him, and to the essential work he did—an everlasting continuance among the possessions of this world."

IV

With Chalmers as Moderator the first Assembly of the Free Church proceeded to business and the new denomination began its active career. Things had been well managed in preparing for the Disruption ; they were now well managed in building up the structure that had to be erected upon that foundation. Committees were appointed, and encouraging reports were received with regard to finance and the provision of buildings for outgoing congregations. Arrangements were made for carrying on the schemes of the Church at home and abroad. Information was forthcoming as to the large proportion of probationers and divinity students who proposed to adhere to the Free Church.

Perhaps the most important transaction in the course of this Assembly was the signing of the Deed of Demission, a document in legal form by which 474 ministers ultimately intimated to the authorities of the Church which they had left that they resigned their benefices and agreed that these be dealt with

H

as vacant. Buchanan records the enthusiasm of one spectator
when, as he puts it, " above four hundred of the best ministers
in the land cheerfully came forward to sacrifice all that was
dear to them in this world on the altar of conscience and duty.'
It had been agreed that Sunday the 21st would be the last
Sunday on which they would conduct worship in their old
churches, and that on the following Sunday they would
simultaneously preach in some other building or in the
open air.

In the enthusiasm of its beginning the new denomination
seemed to have boundless vigour. A great amount of attention
had naturally to be given to finance, a matter that had not
formerly much concerned the Church ; but money in large and
in small sums poured in, and assistance was even received
from America. Churches of simple structure were quickly
erected in hundreds of parishes, for the Free Church meant to
provide ordinances for such as might adhere to it in every
district. Hardship and bitterness of feeling were in certain
areas caused by the refusal of sites by landlords. Parliament
had at length to interfere to prevent this from becoming too
serious ; but for a time some congregations suffered from petty
persecution, as is fully detailed in that most sentimental of
books, Thomas Brown's *Annals of the Disruption*. This has
many a pathetic tale to tell also about farewell services in the
old church, about the minister and his family leaving the
familiar manse, about the surrender of *quoad sacra* buildings
to the Church of Scotland. There was trouble too because
schoolmasters who joined the Free Church were dismissed from
the parish schools which were under kirk-session control. The
Free Church set about erecting schools of its own, and this
duplication at least was no misfortune to the country. Another
ambitious scheme that prospered was the provision of manses.
This matter had been placed under the care of Thomas Guthrie,
and well he justified the choice.

Guthrie was one of the younger Non-intrusionists, over
six feet in height and of commanding appearance, not of the
intellectual type but with a great gift for carrying away the
crowd by his emotional eloquence aided by a strong, musical

roice and easy gestures, rich fancy and a gift for anecdote, one of Edinburgh's favourite preachers and understood by the simplest. An ardent Evangelical, practical, independent, he was an early advocate of the abolition of Patronage, became a popular religious writer, took a leading part in the deputation and agitation work preparatory to the Disruption, and was famous later for his " Ragged Schools."

Perhaps no better account of the Free Church of those early days can be found than one which has become well-known through being quoted by Principal Rainy. It speaks of " the peculiar glow, the moral elevation and exhilaration of the years which succeeded the Disruption," and it continues : " In the case of many good men, who had taken risk and suffered loss for a cause which they deemed to be the cause of Christ, this was nothing else than the spirit of glory and of God resting on them. In the case of many who were not so spiritual, it was the contagious enthusiasm which a worthy cause, guided by high-hearted leaders, always propagates through the ranks of its adherents. In the case of the Church generally, it was the feeling of sympathy with a great movement : a movement believed to be authenticated from on high, felt also to be borne on below by whatever in the Church was manly, generous and self-forgetting. People who are themselves no heroes feel, in being associated with such a movement, a touch of the heroic, which elevates and expands them. Mingling with all this, there was much humility, prayer, gratitude, dependence on God, expectation, and hope. In the skirts of it there was no doubt a good deal of pride, vanity and assumption. We were, I fear, rather intolerable to the other churches in those days, as a company lost in mutual gratulations. Yet with all our faults, the mode of feeling which prevailed among us was not in the main unworthy. No Free Churchman who shared it will ever think so. It was an experience never to be forgotten ; always to be gratefully looked back upon. It made men capable of larger thoughts and greater deeds, and more willing endurance. It will abide with us till we die, as one of the things for the sake of which a man is glad to have lived. And it was attended, as I say, with a singular glow and exhilaration.

It was a kind of ' mount,' from which we had no wish and no
intention to come down."

V

The Non-intrusion leaders had well prepared and well
staged the party procedure on the day of the Disruption ; and
there was much that was romantic and soul-stirring about the
drama. The narrative of the proceedings of those who were
left to constitute the Assembly of the Church of Scotland in
St Andrew's Church is much more prosaic. The Moderate
party had for a generation been on the wane, and it was not to
be expected that it would in the emergency produce a John
Forbes of Corse, a Principal Robertson or a " Jupiter " Carlyle.
Its leaders, Dr George Cook, the ageing Dr Mearns, James
Robertson of Ellon, Principal Macfarlan of Glasgow, Dr Bryce
from Calcutta, Professor Hill of Glasgow, Bisset of Bourtie,
Pirie of Dyce, Paull of Tullynessle, were all men of some weight ;
but they could scarcely be said to rank with the outstanding
figures in the other party, and although the Assembly retained
the intelligent and spiritually minded representatives of the
Middle party, these might be regarded at the moment as
occupying the front opposition benches rather than cabinet
seats.

Principal Macfarlan had been Moderator of the General
Assembly as far back as 1819 when minister of Drymen. The
Assembly of 1824 agreed to his holding the ministerial charge of
Glasgow Cathedral along with the Principalship of the adjacent
University. In 1835 Macfarlan was responsible for the
initiation of the Colonial work of the Church. Dr Bryce is
described as young-looking for his age, active, fidgety, smiling,
speaking clearly and thinking clearly, yet not particularly
influential as his Moderatism was that of an earlier generation.
A memorandum sent by him from India in 1824 was instrumental in leading to the appointment of the first missionary of
the Church, Dr Alexander Duff. Bryce published various
pamphlets in connection with the Non-intrusion controversy
and his history of the Disruption from the Moderate point of

view, though it is dull beside the equally biassed but picturesque Buchanan, includes an excellent introductory sketch of Scottish Church History. Dr Alexander Hill, son of the more distinguished theological teacher, the Moderate leader, Principal George Hill of St Andrews, was a sound scholar, an efficient professor and an authority on Church Law. He had the honour of being preferred to Dr Chalmers for the Glasgow chair in 1840.

The Assembly had not, like that in Tanfield Hall, a prepared programme of procedure, and almost all that could have been expected of them was to keep the maimed Church in being until means could be devised to bring it back to health and usefulness. It was inevitable that with the departure of such a very considerable number of the Evangelical party with their great leaders, control of the constitutional Church of Scotland Assembly would lie with the chief Moderates, and indeed with the more reactionary among these. Dr Cook was thus able to win approval for the course which he had consistently advocated. Such measures of Assembly during the past ten years as had been declared by the highest legal authorities to have been illegally enacted were not rescinded, but merely ignored. If the Church courts were incompetent to pass a particular act, that act could not be said to have been passed, and so the position was precisely as before the act was proposed. It had been decreed, for example, that the Assembly acted *ultra vires* in the case of the Veto, and hence what they did had no legal binding force, and there was therefore nothing to undo. Any group of people might make a rule, but if they had no right to do so, no court would recognize their rule, and it would be to all intents non-existent. Moderates could not admit that the Veto Act, being unconstitutional, had ever been the law of the Church. To admit so much would even have amounted to admitting themselves liable to censure or excommunication for things they had done. The Chapel Act was dealt with in this same manner, and in consequence charges of this class which remained in the Church of Scotland were for the time being reduced to their former unsatisfactory dependent position. Similarly the Strathbogie Seven were not reponed, but treated as if no legal sentence had been pronounced against them. Members of the Middle party opposed this procedure, having at the time believed the acts to be legal and having voted for them. They would have liked officially to undo what had been officially, if mistakenly, done by the majority in former Assemblies. But all were agreed that until the Legislature intervened, the situation was as stated by the law courts. The more extreme Moderates did not consider that any change in the law was needed ; but the opinion prevailed that the trend of the times required that the people's existing right to offer objection to a presentee must be more clearly defined and more generously interpreted, and one result was the Scotch Benefices Bill promoted by Lord Aberdeen. This permitted parishioners to offer objections " of any kind " to a presentee, and the Presbytery in judging of these to take into consideration the whole circumstances of the parish, the spiritual welfare and edification of the congregation and the number and character of the objectors. This compromise Act was only moderately successful, and no doubt the Church's experience of it was one of the influences which ultimately led it to accept the repeal of the 1712 Act. Next year an Act was passed by Parliament to facilitate the dividing of extensive or populous parishes and the erection of parishes *quoad sacra* on condition of certain endowments being procured. Thus the chief advantages sought by the Chapel Act were made ultimately available by amicable arrangement between Church and State, and James Robertson's magnificent work for Church Extension provided one of the most encouraging features of the new period.

Before the Non-intrusionists departed from St Andrew's Church on the day of the Disruption, Dr Welsh had laid on the table the *Protest* which he had just read. It was not presented to any constituted body and might therefore have been ignored ; but the Assembly of the Church of Scotland thought that it called for a reply, and a committee was appointed to this end. Discussion showed that the Middle party held views of Scottish Church History similar to those which the *Protest* assumed. The Moderates, on the other hand, put quite another interpretation upon documents and incidents and laid the emphasis upon totally different aspects of the Church's experience. Nothing at the moment was more important for the damaged Church of Scotland than to hold together the various groups which were ready to co-operate in its continuance and revival ; and it was found inpracticable to frame such an answer to the *Protest* as would satisfy all. The attempt was therefore quietly abandoned. The fact that the *Protest* remained unanswered has sometimes rashly been assumed to imply that it was unanswerable.

Those who held by the old Church had to face tremendous difficulties. The drift of public opinion in that age was clearly against them, and they had every encouragement to develop either an inferiority complex or a hardening and stiffening of heart. Of some of them it was true that, as the *Life of Robert Story* indicates, " gibes and scorn, misrepresentation and calumny were their portion, and to their lasting credit, be it recorded, a portion accepted meekly and without retaliation. There were many who remained to whom it would have been easier to secede, to whom it was harder to stay behind amid reproach and thankless neglect than to go out amid a tumult of popular applause. ' It would have been far easier for me to go than to remain,' said Mr Story."

Similarly, in the *Memoir of Norman Macleod* we read : " ' The sacrifices,' he often said, ' were certainly not all on one side.' With indignant energy he portrayed the trial it was to the flesh to keep by the unpopular side and to act out what conscience dictated as the line of duty. If it was hard to go out, it was harder to stay in. It would have been a relief to have joined the procession of those who passed out amid the huzzas of the populace, and who were borne on the tide of enthusiasm, greeted as martyrs and regarded as saints, in place of remaining by the apparent wreck of all that was lately a prosperous Church."

The prospects for the Church of Scotland were not bright. Some critics were satisfied that it simply could not survive in its crippled condition. Cunningham said, " The idea of the residuary Establishment doing anything valuable towards promoting the salvation of souls is perfectly ridiculous." In

those days Norman Macleod could only go so far as to say:
" We may survive."

There was a complete break between those who stayed and
those who went.   Candlish declared : " No faithful member of
the Free Protesting Church of Scotland can give any countenance
to the worship of God in connection with the Establishment."
Hugh Miller made his celebrated utterance that the parish
minister was " the one excommunicated man of the district,
the man with whom no one is to join in prayer."   It is scarcely
possible to exaggerate the bitterness of feeling that was generated
and that long remained.

To find ministers to fill the hundreds of vacant pulpits was
no easy task, and the places of pious and able and zealous men
had sometimes to be taken by men less highly qualified.   Fortunately there were at the period very many probationers of the
Church acting as teachers and in other secular positions, and
these were soon in demand.   The Free Church in its endeavour
to plant a church in every parish experienced a similar difficulty.
The Reformation, the Restoration and the Revolution Settlement
had all produced this same problem.   In some districts the
Church of Scotland found itself almost completely deserted ;
in others the Disruption made relatively little impression ;
but about a third of the membership of the Church as a whole
went out in 1843.   What happened in particular parishes
depended to some extent upon the character and popularity of
the minister.

In due course it became evident that the Church of Scotland
was not merely to survive, but that it was making an excellent
recovery and gathering strength.   Indeed, it revived in truly
amazing fashion.   It continued, of course, to possess everywhere
churches, manses, schools and stipends.   It had also the
framework of the Five Schemes, which were immediately and
successfully resumed.   It had the traditions of centuries behind
it.   It retained the affection of a multitude even of those who
were careless about religious ordinances.   It attracted by its
moderation, its unexcited, tolerant, patient, commonsense
attitude to life.   There was also the impression that the agitation,
like most agitations, had been overdone, that the problem had

been exaggerated, that zeal had carried people much further than they had intended to go, that words had assumed undue importance, that a little more forbearance all round might have preserved the Church from schism, and that perhaps when passions cooled and reflection supervened, the day might come when brethren would again dwell together in unity.

CHAPTER VII

THE SEPARATE WITNESS

I

THE period from 1850 was one of such rapid change and development in many departments of life and thought that it is not possible to speak of it as a whole with any accuracy. At the beginning of it Cockburn could say : " Britain is at present an island of lunatics, all railway mad " ; but what an advance there has been in railroad transport since those days ! The cab, too, gave way to the taxi, the horse tram to the motor 'bus. What improvements have taken place in ship-building ! And now we have the aeroplane and the submarine. For the lighting of streets electricity has gradually ousted gas as gas ousted oil. Towns and cities have expanded, and produced not only modern police and water supply and hospitals, but also slums and a brood of new and lively social problems. The excitement of the annual fair has been replaced by the routine of the nightly cinema. The post office has developed into a great institution and keeps adding to its functions. Since the Exhibition of 1851 the gross wealth of Britain has vastly increased and the general standard of living risen. Industry has multiplied its efforts, and correspondingly the world has more and more poured its supplies into the country.

Imperial History supplied the episodes of the Crimea and the Mutiny, with later Egyptian campaigns and, at the turn of the century, the Boer War. Life at home felt the influence of Garibaldi's campaigns, the American Civil War and Lincoln, the Franco-Prussian War and Bismarck, besides minor conflicts like that of the United States with Spain and that of Russia with Japan. Politics produced the dominant personalities of Disraeli and Gladstone, the Irish problem, the Free Trade controversy ; nor should the personal influence of Queen Victoria be overlooked. The franchise was extended by the Second Reform Act of 1867, and there were later extensions, further steps in the steady progress of the industrial classes to influence and the democratization of institutions. Education had become more widespread, making good progress in Scotland after it passed under State control ; buildings, educational policy and curriculum, the position and qualifications of teachers being altered almost beyond recognition since 1872. Trade Unionism, Socialism, the Independent Labour Party, Fabianism, Old Age Pensions, the National Insurance Act, the first Labour Government, the General Strike, Communism—these phrases indicate a radical change in the balance of power within the community. Henry George, the Webbs, Karl Marx, H. G. Wells are amongst the names that stand out in connection with social change. In the twentieth century the emancipation of women made rapid strides. Mill's *Essay on Liberty* had appeared as early as 1859. In the same year a new era in world outlook may be said to have begun with the publication of Darwin's *Origin of Species*. Huxley and Herbert Spencer set the fashion of scepticism and a materialistic view of the Universe. Science as the servant of the community brought forth telegraph and telephone, photography, X-rays, anæsthetics, discovery after discovery, invention after invention, until wonder has almost vanished. History, psychology, economics, groped their way to the status of sciences, and specialism became an outstanding feature of the intellectual world. In philosophy one of the strongest influences in Scotland had been that of Hegelianism. German thought assumed increasing importance as the century advanced, and no province was more deeply affected than Theology. The Oxford Movement continued to have a stirring power in England, with slight repercussions north of the Border, but there more influence could be attributed to early Broad Church thinkers such as Coleridge, Maurice and Stanley. In Literature great names included those of the poets Tennyson, Browning, Matthew Arnold, Swinburne and the novelists Dickens, Thackeray, George Eliot, Trollope, Meredith and Hardy, fiction being in growing demand and continuing in the twentieth century with undiminished vigour in such writers as Galsworthy, while journalism developed into one of the great powers, to be followed in this respect by broadcasting. In this catalogue Scotland has not been treated by itself. Although in Law and Religion Scotland insisted upon remaining aloof from English ways, the reading and thinking of the two countries were by no means on different lines. In many of the departments also Scotland made a contribution of real value to the common stock, as the following random list of names will testify : J. Y. Simpson, David Brewster, William Ramsay, James Clerk Maxwell, J. G. Frazer, Thomas Carlyle, A. J. Balfour, J. Ramsay Macdonald, George Macdonald, R. L. Stevenson, J. M. Barrie, and David Wilkie.

During the second half of the nineteenth century the Scottish people remained relatively orthodox, Bible-reading and church-going, and maintained a Victorian standard of propriety and respectability, and at least a fashion of godliness. In " these hurrying years " of the new century the situation is different and becoming steadily more so. But until our new age commenced, Scotland, though relatively so very small in population, had three fully equipped Presbyterian Churches working independently side by side, and was ready and able to support them. These denominations, the Church of Scotland, the Free Church and the United Presbyterian Church, had many centuries of common tradition behind them ; they differed on no material theological issue ; in worship and discipline they were nearly indistinguishable. The difference was chiefly tempera- mental, and the concrete expressions of it were sufficiently obvious to those within the Scottish Presbyterian circle ; but those without might be excused for some failure to appreciate their importance. There were not, indeed, three self-contained groups, for decided variety could be traced within each, and each included persons whose position approximated to that of members of one of the other groups. The separation was a matter of degree. Thus Landsborough, who became a good Free Churchman, had written : " In most cases I would from conscience vote with the Moderates, but I would not pledge myself to go through thick and thin with them. I think the Moderates have in general more candour and liberality ; but I am afraid that as a party they are less clerical and have less religion than the other party."

II

As the century advanced, although the three Churches were rivals and remained very critical of one another, they all had the same general conditions to face, and all faced them in a somewhat similar manner. All had an educated ministry ordained by the laying on of the hands of the Presbytery ; all had kirk-sessions, Sunday schools, a service in which the sermon occupied the principal place.

Theology in all three Churches followed the line of the *Westminster Confession*, which they all accepted as their subordinate standard. In the Church of Scotland, teaching was usually conservative, holding fast to Hill's *Lectures in Divinity* ; but the spirit of enquiry was encouraged under John Tulloch, Principal of St Mary's, St Andrews, a broad-minded but at the same time reverent student, who was in touch with English and continental trends of thought and who did useful work in historical theology. John Macleod Campbell's great book on the *Nature of the Atonement*, published in 1856, long after his deposition at the hands of the stricter party in the pre-Disruption Church, had considerable influence, affecting such men as Norman Macleod. John Caird was strongly under Hegelian impressions, " was almost indifferent to the causes of disagreement between the main denominations into which the Christian Church is divided," and was less concerned about dogma than about practical Christianity. The volume entitled *Scotch Sermons* (1880) was a further indication of a tendency to shake loose from scholastic Calvinism. Robert Flint, erudite and scholarly, was another man of modern outlook who exercised wide influence from his chair in the University of Edinburgh.

The Free Church began in enthusiastic orthodoxy, for its existence was due to a movement to maintain what were regarded as ancient features of the Scots Kirk threatened by the new times. The bi-centenary of the Westminster Assembly in the summer of 1843 was made the occasion of emphasizing the loyalty of the newly formed denomination to Westminster standards. William Cunningham's work was " consistent and uncompromising Presbyterian Calvinistic dogma." One of the main obstacles to union with the U.P. Church in the period 1863-73 was the suspicion on the part of Begg and his friends that orthodoxy might be endangered. The Robertson Smith case resulting in the professor's removal from his Aberdeen chair by the Assembly of 1881 under Rainy's leadership, revealed a strong body of feeling against the Biblical critical methods associated with such names as Wellhausen. But the cause so unhappily represented by this young master of Semitics soon gained ground from the support consistently given to it by men of high intellectual and spiritual standing like T. M. Lindsay, and latterly the Free Church produced a brilliant succession of advanced teachers who justly brought it world-distinction. Two of these, George Adam Smith and Marcus Dods, had to face heresy trials ; but public opinion in the Free Church had shifted its centre and they were exonerated, and the whole Church learned to be proud of them and of James Denney, A. B. Davidson, A. B. Bruce and James Moffatt. In 1892 a Declaratory Act anent the *Westminster Confession* emphasized liberty of conscience and the right of private judgment, and somewhat relaxed the dogmatic strictness of an earlier period. A small section of the Church in the Highlands seceded on this account and came to be known as the Free Presbyterian Church, and a similar view continued within the Free Church among those who in 1900 were to become the so-called " Wee Frees."

It was in the United Presbyterian Church that the earliest signs of liberal theology emerged. This denomination was independent of State restraint, and though the Seceders had, to begin with, left the Church of Scotland partly on account of evidences of theological laxity, and though the United Secession Church felt it necessary in 1841 to suspend James Morison for revolt from certain prevailing Calvinistic teachings, the Relief Church had shown a liberal spirit ; and the U.P. Church, in which they combined, was led by John Cairns as early as 1879 to pass a Declaratory Act giving liberty of opinion on matters " not entering into the substance of the faith." Cairns, who became Principal of the U.P. Divinity Hall, was great physically, intellectually and spiritually ; and though he left little in print and was himself a traditionist, his personality impressed his own denomination and others, and was an encouragement to liberty and charity. John Eadie was amongst the scholars entrusted with the work of producing the Revised Version. At a later date James Orr was the outstanding representative of a conservative party in theology:

Those in the three Churches who were skilled in doctrine went through somewhat similar Arts courses in the Scottish Universities, perused the same theological text-books, faced the same theological controversies, and moved gradually in the same direction of deeper and broader scholarship and knowledge, a fuller understanding of the Bible, a truer conception of History, a better sense of proportion in doctrinal matters and a wider tolerance.

All three Churches followed much the same order of public worship and observed in a similar manner the Sacraments of Baptism and the Lord's Supper. For some time only Metrical Psalms were employed in most churches, though the Paraphrases had also a certain popularity. Instrumental music was not tolerated, and the singing, led by the precentor, while hearty, had often little of the melodious about it. Choirs had begun to appear in some town churches. There were generally only two items of praise, and these the minister read through from beginning to end. The people remained seated while they sang. For the prayers the congregation stood. The lengthy sermon was the chief feature of the occasion. It was the general custom for ministers to memorize their sermons : John Caird did this with great effect ; but reading was becoming commoner after the example of Chalmers, Thomas Guthrie and John Brown of Broughton Place. The U.P. Church in 1849, by a small majority, passed a resolution against the practice of reading sermons. All three Churches had eminent preachers ; for example, Norman Macleod, Alexander Whyte, John Ker. The use of hymns was begun by the Relief Church and a U.P. Hymn Book appeared in 1851. The Church of Scotland followed ten years later. Instrumental music was in many quarters strenuously opposed and was only very gradually introduced. A harmonium made its appearance in Greyfriars'

Parish Church, Edinburgh, in 1863, and an organ a few years later. Instrumental music was rejected by the U.P. Synod in 1856 but permitted in 1872. In the Free Church R. S. Candlish had firmly held that the introduction of organs would be followed by a return of Romish ritual, but in 1883 the Assembly agreed that there was nothing in the Word of God or in the constitution and laws of the Church to preclude the use of instrumental music in public worship as an aid to vocal praise. Some parts of the country long declined to follow such a lead. There is at least one Parish Church to-day which has never had instrumental music, while both hymns and organs are rejected by the present Free Church. In the 'seventies we find the change of posture being introduced here and there, and except in some of the smaller Presbyterian denominations, congregations have long stood to sing and remained seated during the prayers. Prayers were extemporaneous though not always very varied from Sunday to Sunday. It was not till the second half of the century that special attention was called to the importance of order and decency in religious worship, and the need for some study of liturgical literature by those who were to lead the prayers of the people. The Church of Scotland led in this movement, and Robert Lee was the first to attract notice for " innovations." Very considerable progress has since been made, the idea of worship being emphasized, services being more reverent, church buildings more tasteful, and less cold and uncomfortable, the music more varied and more worthy, the sermon less dominating and the prayers more carefully planned. Calvin and Knox were puritan in their suspicion of aids to devotion, but they would have been astonished at the bareness of Scottish churches and services in the early nineteenth century. Worship has since been assisted by the publication of volumes by groups in each of the Churches for the guidance of ministers, and though the warmth of free prayer is greatly prized there is less prejudice against the reading of prayers. The Lord's Prayer, which, for historical reasons, long suffered neglect, is returning to the place Knox gave it ; and the chief dates of the Christian Year, which were so heartily condemned in the reign of James VI, have been restored to notice. Amongst those who have had a special part in encouraging a dignified and orderly worship were Dr Bisset of Bourtie ; Dr John Macleod of Govan ; Dr Sprott and Professor James Cooper. All the three Churches have moved in one direction though at different rates.

Early in the nineteenth century the practice began of the whole congregation taking Communion simultaneously instead of at successive tables ; in most places the white cloths on the pews were the only relic of the older custom, and tents were no longer necessary outside for the additional sermons to the waiting crowds.

Closely allied to the subject of worship is the problem of Sunday observance. Public opinion in Scotland was particularly obstinate with regard to strictness in keeping the " Sabbath," as it was very generally called in this period. English influence slowly worked a change, and in 1865 Sunday trains were introduced as in the south. Churchmen broke into opposition and a pamphlet warfare started. The sensation of the time was that Norman Macleod took a pronounced position against Sabbatarianism, seeking to dissociate the Lord's Day from mere Judaism. In the Free Church and U.P. Church there were more of such external evidences of piety as prayer meetings ; perhaps also more general observance of family prayers. Recent times have witnessed the decay of such traditional practices and the problem of Sunday observance has become steadily more complicated and difficult.

III

In the province of Church Government the three Churches differed in matters of detail. Thus in the Church of Scotland the finances were controlled by the Session ; in the Free Church by a Deacons' Court including minister and elders ; and under the more democratic constitution of the U.P. Church by a Committee of Management with a lay preses, the minister not being an *ex officio* member. Again, while membership of the General Assemblies of the Church of Scotland and the Free Church was representative, the Synod of the U.P. Church consisted of all ministers with elders from all the congregations. In the U.P. Church the election of the Synod Moderator was actually in the hands of the assembled members, and not previously arranged by some Committee. For a time Committees were appointed in this same independent, but in practice rather haphazard, manner. Much more vital is the matter of the relation of the several Churches to the State. The Church of Scotland was by law established, and enjoyed certain ancient endowments which it regarded as its patrimony or part of what it had once possessed as its own property, especially Teind, which corresponds to Tithe in England, and which brought with it responsibility for offering the Gospel to all upon a territorial basis. The Free Church accepted the principle of Establishment, but regarded itself as outwith State control except with respect to secular affairs, and was from the beginning supported by the voluntary gifts of its members. The U.P. Church utterly rejected any State connection and made a principle of Voluntaryism, though it was never a term of Communion. Laymen had a larger say in this Church's affairs ; property was on a congregational basis ; and liberality was an outstanding feature.

There was certainly a different ethos in the three Churches, but all changed their position with the course of time, and the differences tended to lessen. The Church of Scotland had little at any time of the Erastianism of John Hope. The general view heartily accepted the benefits and opportunities of establishment and thought that these outweighed any difficulties due to the compromises inevitable when two powers negotiate. It was regarded as only the duty of the Church to obey the law, but, where required, to press for reform and to exercise as strong an influence as possible upon the community as a whole and those who governed it. Thus the Church of Scotland acquiesced in Patronage, which no one regarded as a faultless system, but which many preferred to any other proposed ; but as time went on, the system became more and more irksome to the ordinary church member. This was owing partly to the growth of democratic principles, to the fact that the members of the dissenting churches had on this point a privilege which members of the Church of Scotland lacked, and to the experience within the Church of Scotland of the working of an increasing number of *quoad sacra* churches erected to supply ordinances in crowded districts or communities distant from the old church. In these the congregation had the choice of a minister and paid most of the stipend as if under Voluntary conditions. Not many months after the Disruption we already find Norman Macleod writing : " I rather think the struggle against Patronage is to be renewed and that twenty years will see its death." The Scotch Benefices Act of 1843 had been a source of fairly frequent irritation and litigation, and in 1866 the Assembly appointed a Committee to consider the modification of the present law of Patronage. Dr Pirie of Dyce was as a result able to carry the Assembly with him in favour of abolition, and Parliament was approached. There was opposition from the few extreme Moderates, from Free Church leaders and most of all from the Voluntaries. Free Churchmen were emphatic that the removal of Patronage would not provide that spiritual independence the refusal of which led to the Disruption. Gladstone, as Prime Minister, was not very friendly ; but in 1874 he had to make way for Disraeli, and soon a Bill was before Parliament and became law. It was not intended as an undoing of the Disruption, but as an attempt to bring the Church of Scotland up to date. Incidentally, however, it showed that the State need not be regarded as necessarily hostile to the well-being of the Church, and the success of the method of negotiation and constitutional procedure in this case was certainly a good augury for the future. Also it did at last bring all these three Churches into line on this subject of long and bitter controversy ; and though as rivals they remained suspicious and jealous of one another, the differences that were not temperamental were at least beginning to fade away.

The Free Church had at first been ostentatiously definite in its rejection of Voluntaryism. Chalmers in particular had made emphatic statements, and Candlish had hotly denied that the movement was " at all a step in advance to the Voluntary principle." But it may be noted that Thomas Guthrie was more clear-sighted as to the drift of things, for already in 1843 he said : " Rest assured we shall change our views on that question. No non-established Church can long keep clear of what is called Voluntaryism. Thirty years will alter all our convictions." In 1876 Lord Ardmillan, in the introduction to *Disruption Worthies*, wrote : " The Church is freer, safer and purer, when depending only on the freewill offerings of the Christian people." The Free Church as a result of experience was moving towards the Voluntary position.

What Chalmers and others disliked about the Voluntaries was their individualism. They were not interested in the National Recognition of Religion or any duty of the organized community to profess concern for religion or support religious ordinances. Chalmers firmly believed in State establishment of religion, and one of the most important obligations of the Church seemed to him to be the provision of the Gospel for those who did not want it and were not prepared to pay for it. He would have had everyone given an opportunity to worship. He would have had Christianity everywhere aggressively thrusting itself upon people's notice. He believed it to be the State's business thus indirectly through the Church to prevent the emergence of social evils and to remove such as were already blotting the social landscape. He was tremendously worried by the amount of non-churchgoing that was due, not to hostility but to indifference and lack of encouragement and friendly guidance. He felt that much of this could be counteracted if taken in time, but that the indifferent would soon become the hostile if no effort were made to win their interest, and he was certain that only a National Church with adequate resources and independence could be expected to face the task.

The Voluntaries were not only believers in self-support. They were believers in spiritual independence, and felt this to be out of the question if and when any outside body such as Government had power to interfere. They also objected to privilege, and protested against the favoured position which the Established Church had inherited from the centuries, but which was contrary to the doctrine of religious equality and which was not so easy to justify now that the Church of Scotland could no longer claim as members anything like the whole body of the citizens. Voluntaries worked on congregational lines, each church building being owned by the congregation and not by the denomination. Centralization such as the Free Church deliberately planned under its Sustentation Fund was rejected. They further objected to the low standard of church membership and giving, which establishment and endowment seemed to encourage ; and they preferred a congregation to consist of a small group of consecrated Christians stimulating one another and acting as a leaven in society, rather than of everyone who was willing to come under the guidance and to accept the ministrations of the Church. In many respects they had close affinity with English Nonconformists. But in spite of its inherent congregationalism and individualism, the U.P. Church showed itself eagerly missionary, and the strong learned to help the weak.

The care of the poor had always been a principal concern of the Scottish Church, which endeavoured to meet the most urgent needs of each parish mainly from the free-will offerings of the people. There was no real attempt to solve such problems as those presented by unemployment or the sturdy beggar, and emigration had too often been the only course open to the unfortunate. But orphans and incurables, the destitute aged and the victims of disaster were kept from starvation, and the system afforded every opportunity for personal contact between the paupers and those who cared for them. Chalmers was a resolute defender of this tradition, and sought to vindicate it by his Glasgow experiment ; but the industrial revolution had materially altered the whole conditions of society, and it came to be fairly generally agreed that the problem of poverty must be faced on a national scale with the aid of compulsory taxation, even if this did involve secularization. The Disruption helped to give the last blows to the old system, for the collections in Free Churches were required for the support of ministers, buildings and schemes, and the Parish Church collection plate suffered badly through the loss of the offerings of those who went out. The State took over the care of the poor in 1845.

Education was another of the important matters over which the Church had maintained control since the Reformation.

This was also to slip from her keeping, with results of which the country is not even yet fully cognizant. But for a time after the Disruption education improved, for the Free Church set itself the ideal of erecting a Free Church school in every parish. This not only increased the facilities by multiplying buildings and masters, but it introduced a new spirit of rivalry between sessions and between teachers which must have had some effect on the standard. In those circumstances, not only did direct religious instruction familiarize the children with the contents of the Bible, the answers in the Shorter Catechism and the tunes of the Psalms, but as the masters were in many cases men who were or had been looking forward to the ministry, the whole education had a religious basis, and the policy behind education throughout the country had not yet fallen into confusion. Incidentally, teachers often directed promising pupils to the ministry as a profession, and the standard of candidates remained high and the supply ample : this was a contributory feature in the strength of the Church in the period. The secularization process had, however, set in before the Disruption, partly by reason of the activities of dissenting bodies ; and among the Voluntaries there was, indeed, a strong sentiment that, as in religion so in education, people should pay for what they want, and the State should not grant to any denomination a position of privilege even in the matter of responsibility. The long controversy with regard to the foundation of an Academy at Peterhead, independent of the National Church and of denominational religious teaching, was significant.

This same attitude showed itself in connection with University education, for there the Church of Scotland had again a position of traditional privilege. At the Disruption the Free Church toyed with the idea of an institution separate from the University of Edinburgh to provide a course in Arts and Divinity ; but this was soon recognized to be impracticable, and attention turned rather to the removal of existing restrictions affecting scholars outwith the Church of Scotland. There had, indeed, been some informality in the matter already ; but in 1852 the ecclesiastical test was abolished except in the case of theological professorships. William Cunningham and John Cairns played some part in this campaign. Long afterwards Cairns supported a proposal to have the test abolished also in the Divinity Faculty, but it was only after the Union of 1929 that this was partially effected. In the second half of the century Scotland certainly had ample provision for the training of candidates for the ministry. The four Universities had Divinity Faculties where the students of the Church of Scotland were prepared. The Free Church on its formation at once began theological instruction at Edinburgh, and later Colleges were added at Aberdeen and Glasgow. The United Presbyterian Church had its Divinity Hall in Edinburgh. From the scientific point of view there has been considerable improvement in the range of teaching, and there is a real concern to keep abreast of the times and to fit men to meet the needs of the times.

IV

Each of the three Churches had its own characteristics, and those intimate with the conditions could distinguish a minister of one from a minister of another by slight differences in dress, manner and outlook, and a less or more puritan attitude to certain amusements and social habits. Each of the Churches had its personalities. Some of these have already been mentioned, but amongst others belonging to the Church of Scotland must be remembered Principal W. R. Pirie of Aberdeen, who was one of the younger Moderates at the Disruption, later stood out against the innovations of Lee, had his name associated with the Act of 1865 which has been the basis of policy on this matter ever since, and finally was one of the chief agents in obtaining the abolition of Patronage ; A. H. Charteris, Professor of Biblical Criticism at Edinburgh, a particularly active pioneer in practical developments, initiating the Christian Life and Work Committee and the Woman's Guild ; A. K. H. Boyd, of St Andrews, who was in a class by himself for interesting talk and contributions to light literature ; and George Matheson, the blind preacher and author of a well-known hymn. Outstanding figures in the Free Church included Dr John

Macdonald of Urquhart, "the Apostle of the North"; Alexander Duff, the first Foreign Missionary sent out by the Church of Scotland ; Horatius Bonar, several of whose hymns are sung in Scottish churches ; and, most prominent of the post-Disruption leaders, Robert Rainy, Principal of New College from 1874 until his death in 1906, for long exercising "undisputed supremacy," "a great opportunist," "comprehensively cautious," "the strongest and wisest of his time," a leader of statesmanship and vision, who through triumph and crisis calmly guided the Free Church and was the hero of many vital incidents in its history. Laymen worthy of note were numerous, but we may mention Sheriff Graham Speirs, D. M. M. Crichton, and John Hamilton. The U.P. Church had, besides those already named, such notables as Principal Harper, methodical and energetic, a man of sound intellect and trusted judgment ; and Duncan McLaren, a keen layman, a man of strong opinions and high idealism.

In this half-century there was tremendous spiritual activity in Scotland—churches and church-goers in plenty, prayer meetings and fruit soirees, revivals and missionary campaigns, family prayers and private Bible-reading, religious periodicals and ecclesiastical pamphlets, Sabbath schools and Bible classes, and the building of halls to house new organizations. The three Churches had their Home, Foreign, Jewish, Colonial and Education schemes, and others were added as means permitted and interest demanded. The Church of Scotland had its Endowment Scheme, adding many new parishes under the stimulus of James Robertson's enthusiasm. The Free Church had its Sustentation Fund, the subject of many a heated Assembly debate, but a wonderful achievement ; and the U.P. Church had a flourishing Augmentation Fund. Norman Macleod nobly served the cause of Home Missions in his extensive Glasgow parish, and under the Free Church there was work at the West Port and Fountainbridge in Edinburgh and in the Wynds of Glasgow. Abroad the Church of Scotland built up healthy mission stations in India, Africa and China, and the Foreign Mission zeal of the Free and U.P. Churches became proverbial throughout Christendom, the work increasing in extent and improving in method and providing both a challenge and a training ground for Union.

The three Churches were in fact in their own ways tackling much the same problems, dealing with much the same types of needy souls, studying much the same literature and seeking much the same ends. There was room for them all, for it was a time when there was plenty of money, when healthy interests were comparatively few, when respectability was fashionable, and when the religious tradition of the past was still a powerful influence. The many congregations offered opportunities of service to many workers ; and the bedding-out process provided by the separate denominations gave room for the characteristic virtues of all three to develop side by side.

At the same time they influenced one another. For long a Parish minister and a Free Church minister could have no dealings with one another, would not even salute one another on the street. But a gradual change of atmosphere took place, and in the end it has turned out to be a better atmosphere than could have been expected apart from the controversies and rivalries and hostilities and misunderstandings. There was still a long way to go before there could be hope of " one face " of Presbyterianism in Scotland, but already there was the belief that Unity must be God's Will, and the nineteenth century, though it witnessed much ecclesiastical disputing, saw also the beginnings of a real movement in that direction. The formation of the United Secession Church in 1820, and that of the United Presbyterian Church in 1847, as well as later unions in Australia and in Canada, were sources of encouragement.

In 1863 the U.P. Church put forward proposals to the Free Church with a view to union, John Cairns being a prominent advocate of this course. Although the two bodies had common ground in their Evangelical principles, the attempt proved to be premature, for a considerable party in the Free Church had difficulties about the more liberal theological attitude of the U.P. Church and also about its pronounced Voluntaryism. By 1869 a campaign against Union was in full swing under the leadership of James Begg of Newington, who had distinguished himself in connection with progressive social work, but who latterly devoted himself to upholding the original 1843 Free Church position. He was strengthened by considerable Highland support, led by John Kennedy of Dingwall, whose Celtic eloquence and evangelical fervour gave him wide influence. Finally, in 1873, the scheme of Union had to be temporarily abandoned.

Leaders of the two Churches, however, found themselves brought into very close association : first in opposing the Church of Scotland's proposal to abandon Patronage, and then in connection with the Disestablishment campaigns. In this last movement democratic opinions on religious equality and wider acceptance of the Voluntary principle helped to stir up what became a fierce and bitter struggle, carried on chiefly in the sphere of party politics. The Church of Scotland was roused to the defence of its privileges and principles, and certainly was the better of the experience. The effort to disestablish the Church of Scotland failed, but the conflict brought out the importance of certain difficulties in the way of final Union, and all parties came to realize that a worthy unity would be reached neither by absorption nor by elimination but only by comprehension.

The U.P. Church gave another invitation in 1896, and negotiations with the Free Church were soon resumed and terms of Union rapidly and harmoniously adjusted. There was no opposition in the former body, but in the latter the same element that had previously stood in the way was once more in evidence, and eventually stayed out of the Union. The United Free Church came into being in 1900 by the incorporation of the two great evangelical Presbyterian denominations, and a very strong Church it formed—high-principled, enterprising, generous, zealous, intelligent, loyal to the past but alive to the present, doing splendid work in theology and preaching and pastoral care, through organizations, through fostering interest in good causes, and by evangelism at home and abroad.

But the Free Church which had so much cause, both in connection with its origin and in the Cardross case, to examine carefully into the powers and responsibilities of the law courts and the fundamental conditions of life within the framework of an organized State, was again to find its actions questioned by the competent authority. Those who resisted the Union did so in the conviction that to unite with the U.P. Church implied the abandonment of the 1843 platform, and that the departure constituted a change of identity. The Union party won its case in the Court of Session, but on appeal to the House of Lords that decision was, by a majority, reversed in 1904. Whether or not this judgment was justified by history and law, it had to be faced, and in a heroic spirit it was faced, and became indeed a " vitalising judgment." A Royal Commission eventually distributed the property concerned in the interests of commonsense, and the trouble no doubt did something to cement the Union ; but the United Free Church had been made thoroughly aware that no property-holding corporation can claim to be free in all the extent of that word. The State, it was obvious, must have the regulation of matters in so far as they may involve contract, and any special liberty claimed must be negotiated and legally guaranteed. Establishment was thus not incompatible with spiritual independence : spiritual independence was not incompatible with establishment ; but the meaning of the words must be kept clear. The exciting legal episode of the Church case made plain the lines upon which alone any future union would be possible, and helped to prevent mere words from being the obstacles which they have so often proved themselves to be in the way of progress. Principal Rainy, with his "charming humility," " hopeful energy," " ripe wisdom " and " pure aspirations," led nobly in both the Union and the Case.

A more comprehensive and epoch-making Union was to follow. In 1907 the Church of Scotland raised the question of union with the United Free Church, and " unrestricted conference upon the whole ecclesiastical situation " was heartily begun. The process of learning to understand one another's vocabulary and trust one another was slow, but step by step difficulties were overcome, and finally, on 2nd October 1929, the Union was consummated. The path had been prepared to some extent by the abolition of Patronage in 1874 ; by the Parliamentary declaration in 1905 of the right of the Church of

Scotland to revise its credal formula ; by the abandonment of a disestablishment policy ; and by the fact of the large number of *quoad sacra* congregations in the Church of Scotland accustomed to Voluntary methods.

The whole situation was different from what it had once been in Scotland. There were no political complications. The totalitarian issue was not yet serious. The Government saw no danger of revolution such as had been possible in Chartist days. English eyes were not half-blinded as in 1843 by a home problem like the Oxford Movement. The State officially was perhaps less interested, but it was more considerate. Men had wider notions of the meaning of Liberty and truer views of the purpose of Law. The Church of Scotland was allowed to state its constitution and had this recognized and registered. Not so easy, indeed, was it to arrange about finance, for in this practical province vested interests were watchful, and in the end the Church had to be content with a less satisfactory compromise than might have been possible, and incidentally sacrificed an appreciable part of its income. Public opinion generally was all for the Union and the removal of the absurdities of duplication in the religious life of such a small country ; and individuals who quite frankly disliked the people and ways of the neighbour Church were yet ready to submit to what they realized was right as well as inevitable.

Time had had its influence upon the problem of Church and State. It was no longer important for the State to take a direct interest in Church affairs in order to express and enforce the will of the Christian community as a check upon clericalism, part of the ultimate significance of Erastianism. Church of Scotland leaders were now less anxious than their fathers had been about the most direct relations between Church and State, for the modern State was capable at any time of assuming a very different attitude to religion from that to which centuries had accustomed men in Scotland, and the need for securing independence was obvious. On the other hand, the spirit of community was abroad, and in the light of modern psychology and of modern experience people were realizing more than formerly the power of corporate sentiments and the influence of spiritual atmosphere, and so those who had been most individualistic were prepared to encourage what Chalmers had called with approval National Recognition of Religion.

The number of persons still acutely conscious of the points of difference between the two Presbyterian bodies was small. Men had come to be concerned about great world problems, and to look at Scottish affairs in a world-setting with a new sense of proportion, which made it obvious that Christianity was more than Presbyterianism, and Presbyterianism more than denominational emphases. Ordinary people went to a particular church, not so much because it belonged to the Church of Scotland or the United Free Church as because they liked the preacher or the music or the fellowship or the way in which the Sunday school was managed. The separations within Scottish Presbyterianism had lost much of their religious significance.

It seemed to be a waste of time, money and man-power to insist on retaining two corporate bodies where one could manage the work quite as well, if not better. Union would involve no sacrifice of principle. Financially, since there were now so many new ways of spending money, Scotland did not find the same satisfaction as formerly in supporting so many rival denominations. Mission work abroad also demanded unity at home. Further, there were now in Scotland many more non-Presbyterians than formerly, and this helped to draw the Presbyterians closer together. The rapid development of the non-Christian and anti-Christian attitude constituted a challenge which made it almost impossible for the two Churches to remain apart, and indeed proclaimed that there simply must be even wider unions, or at least much closer co-operation amongst the Christian Churches, not only in this or that country but throughout the world. There were plainly some religious problems, as for example the approach to youth, which were such as could not adequately be faced by separate sects. For these and other reasons Union was bound to come.

The War of 1914-18 interrupted the negotiations, but made even plainer the obligation to come together and so better to provide for startling new-world conditions. The Church of Scotland prepared articles declaring its constitution, articles which bore a family resemblance to parts of the *Claim of Right*, and Parliament gave its consent to their adoption, while the U.F. Church recognized that the Church of Scotland, still retaining its position of privilege as a national Church, was now as free as any Church could be. The Church of Scotland also obtained an Act of Parliament which declared its source of income, its churches and manses to be its absolute property, " to be held and used by it in the religious interest of the nation and in the exercise of the powers and liberties set forth in the Articles " ; and the U.F. Church professed itself satisfied with the arrangement. In 1926 the Church of Scotland formally adopted the new constitution ; and the two bodies set themselves to frame a Basis and Plan of Union. Thereafter, with the requisite consent of the required subordinate courts, the Union took place. Those chiefly instrumental in advancing the cause of Union included, on the Church of Scotland side, Dr Archibald Scott, Dr William Mair, Lord Balfour of Burleigh, Dr Wallace Williamson, Dr John White and Lord Sands ; and on the U.F. side, Principal Alexander Martin and Dr R. J. Drummond. The impressive ceremonies connected with the consummation of the Union were attended by King George VI (then Duke of York), as High Commissioner for his father, the first occasion upon which a royal prince has appeared in that capacity at a General Assembly of the Church of Scotland.

Thus did Scotland once again, by the grace of God, have a united and national Presbyterian Church claiming the allegiance of the vast majority of Scottish people, a Church with a fit soul in a fit body, prepared by testing to lead Scotland to fuller and higher and richer well-being. The different traditions in Presbyterian Scotland had come to know and appreciate one another, and to realize that each had something to teach the other, that what was specially valued by one was not incompatible with what was highly cherished by the other. Thus Mercy and Truth, Peace and Righteousness, Charity and Principle were combined. Says Bacon : " Shall we not think that God above, that knows the heart, doth not discern that frail men, in some of their contradictions, intend the same thing, and accepteth of both ? "

CHAPTER VIII

IN UNITY TO DWELL

I

" THE Christian good of the people of Scotland " : this is a well-known expression of Dr Chalmers. It may now safely be declared that the Christian good of the people of Scotland was furthered by the Disruption controversy. That anything of the sort should have had to happen was, indeed, extremely unfortunate ; but the Christian community has not in the end been weakened by the experience. The Church in Scotland has a strength to-day which it could not have attained by a more undisturbed passage through the century, and both those who came out and those who stayed in made their contribution towards the benefits which have been wrung from the bitter dispute.

We have noticed that all through Scottish ecclesiastical history there have been two strains, or complementary parties, of which now one and now the other has had the guiding of the Church's affairs. The pendulum has swung across and has swung back, across and back again. It has been fortunate for Christianity in Scotland that neither direction was ever taken completely without counteracting influence, and that though the dominant party generally acted as if it were the Church of Scotland, time presently revealed that this wonderful institution was always greater than any of its constituent elements.

But an important conclusion must be drawn from the historical survey. The metaphor of the swing of the pendulum may be true but is certainly inadequate, for in Scottish Church History there has been a steady movement including, and above, all the pendulum process. One notices a similar development in the political sphere, and there is no need to be an adherent of any Hegelian dialectic philosophy or theory of inevitable uncoiling in history to believe that there has been genuine progress in the gradual change from absolute monarchy to a condition of things that contains at least the hope of a much richer communal and personal health and happiness under a sound democracy. We have moved in the direction of Liberty. One is very apt to confuse the constant equilibration process with progress, but progress there does seem to have been. The glance we took at social conditions behind the Disruption period gave clear indication of progress in Scotland in the material and cultural departments. The standard of living rose. There was greatly increased control of nature and of circumstances, and this meant a foundation for fuller liberty. The Church was also gradually learning by experience; and though the two parties in a general sense remained, and remain, and will remain, their precise problem has changed from age to age, and has never recurred in the same form. There has been a persistent trend in the direction of true liberty, a liberty much richer because of the continuous struggle. Liberty, we know, is constantly building up law, and rising by means of it to new heights. Every stage reached is confirmed, and becomes the starting-point for progress. Law and order and authority are not in the long-run for the sake of repression, but for the sake of preservation; not to prevent progress, but to avoid regress. We know that without constant restraint Liberty would become licence and lead not to life but to death. Nature dictates both the conservation and the advance; yet we must feel that the advance is nature's last word and final purpose.

At first any attempt to break away from ancient custom is regarded as essentially destructive, and any attempt to prevent it as essentially tyrannical. It has to be discovered that the double process is what really counts. The separate witness of the denominations has been of permanent value, but each was necessary to the other. There is nothing inevitable about the result of such an historical movement. England has been led to a different position from that which Scotland has reached. But Scotland has something in its Church as at present constituted of which it may well be proud as an instrument of spiritual power. Ours is a noble Heritage and we have all the responsibility of those to whom much has been given.

The leaders in one century may look back with curiosity at their spiritual ancestors. The family resemblance will be clear and yet much has really changed. The costume, the manner, the language, the particular concrete problem, these are different ; but something has been learned from age to age. Thus there can be no recurrence either of Aird's Moss or of Magus Muir, of the massacre at Philiphaugh or of the Wigton Martyrs, of the burning of witches or the intolerance of the Solemn League and Covenant, of the fanaticism of James Guthry or the paganism of " Jupiter " Carlyle. Neither to-day could we have either the formal Erastianism of John Hope or the exasperated question of Candlish as to whether the Church of Scotland were a church of Christ at all. But it is not merely that the extremes of both sides have become impossible of recurrence. The whole situation has changed. The centre of balance has shifted. It is proverbial that the radicalism of one age becomes the conservatism of the next. So the whole Church has moved to a stronger faith and a wiser tolerance, and there has been a great deepening and development of the conception of religious liberty.

The Christian good of the people of Scotland has been furthered by the fact of the Disruption and the work of the Free Church. The Deed of Demission, making all allowance for the careful preparation and skilful handling of the occasion, startled the onlooking world by its unexpectedness and amazed by its heroism. Cockburn spoke in something of his judicial capacity when he said of the Disruption : " It is the most honourable fact for Scotland that its whole history supplies." Lord Jeffrey, likewise personally to some extent a spectator, declared : " I am proud of my country ; there is not another country upon earth where such a deed could have been done." Gladstone in 1870 spoke of the Disruption Worthies as " a body to whose moral attitude scarcely any word weaker or lower than that of majesty is, according to the spirit of historical criticism, justly applicable."

England, on the whole, was scarcely alive to the situation,

K

J. G. Lockhart could declare that " the ideas entertained in England respecting the state of religion in Scotland are just as absurd as those which used to be in fashion about the external appearance of that country." Dr Chalmers after some experience pronounced that for the principles at stake in Scotland there was little hope of enlisting the understanding of Englishmen : " They are principles for which they have no taste and no comprehension." The *Liverpool Mail* could compare the General Assembly of 1842 to the Assembly of France during the reign of Robespierre and the reign of terror, and protested that " under this pretended love of liberty, this reverence for the opinions of the unlearned, this tenderness towards souls, the artful agitators of the Church, with cant on their lips, hypocrisy in their professions, and rancorous ambition stirring them on, have succeeded in deluding, exciting and alarming a considerable portion of the people." Sir Henry Craik has written with regard to Chalmers's lectures in London : " The situation proved, if proof were necessary, the slender understanding of Scottish affairs that was possible to an English audience." The Puseyites referred to " the sect of Dissenters established by law in Scotland," which was an unhappy beginning for any appreciation of a situation which involved their own doctrine of spiritual independence. The Church of England generally was to such an extent Erastian in its habit of thought that it could scarcely understand the Scottish Moderates or sympathize with the Evangelicals. Much interest was indeed displayed by Methodists and other Nonconformists, but they were halted by the Scottish Free Church emphasis on Establishment. Those connected with Government (with the possible exception of the Duke of Wellington) failed to grasp the position, and a considerable share of responsibility for the Disruption must be attributed to them. On the other hand, enthusiastic appreciation flowed in from Ireland ; Cunningham's mission to the United States brought money and congratulatory resolutions in plenty ; the German Sydow who was present on 18th May wrote a book on the subject from the evangelical standpoint ; and world evangelical opinion generally was more than sympathetic.

In Scotland enormous spiritual enthusiasm was generated by the Disruption. There was an uprush and outpouring of feeling and energy. Ministers, elders and congregations felt themselves able for anything, as after another Pentecost. Everyone had a cause, a call, a message, a duty. Religion had at its command the full resources of the professing Christian community. Sermons composed themselves, and congregations had a new gift of appreciation; prayer meetings had a fresh appeal and effectiveness; floods of generosity were released; churches, manses and schools were built and the schemes better supported than ever. A spirit of sacrifice was fostered and no sacrifice can be spiritually in vain. This religious revival altered the whole religious temperature of Scotland, for it had marked influence upon all the denominations, and not least on the Church of Scotland. The serious problem of Church Extension simplified itself by the parallel activities of the several Presbyterian churches; missionary effort abroad was extended and intensified; Home Mission work was developed; organizations multiplied; education both in schools and universities was improved; and fresh enthusiasm for theological and Biblical study was produced. The effect of the first enthusiasm in these provinces is still felt. The Disruption gave evidence of what can be done if men are brought under the influence of a compelling idea or interest, and what inexhaustible spiritual resources are actually available for good causes. It was noticeable how ready men were to respond to confident leadership. People are, in fact, fairly easily led: easily led into wrong ways but also to a surprising extent easily led in right paths. They will follow a leader, and this should be remembered by the Church, and less apologetic and more assured leadership provided.

To some extent substantial good was counterbalanced by the extraordinary bitterness produced by the controversy. There were indeed no burnings or massacres and no civil war such as some earlier century might have thought necessary; but there was released an intensity of unfriendly emotion and a ruthlessness of utterance that were quite as dangerous to the community. No quarrels seem to be so acute as those within the Christian

household : religious matters are of such vital importance and
affect the soul so radically that differences exacerbate feelings.
Some of Hugh Miller's inflammatory remarks and sarcastic
reports may have been good journalistic propaganda, but they
were so far from the Christian spirit that a newspaper writer
of the time declared that nothing could do more harm in the
mission-field than a few pages of the *Witness*.   Dr Alexander
Duff at Calcutta also used very exaggerated language, and
both Candlish and Cunningham said extremely bitter things.
Throughout the country local politics, and local trade and local
friendships were affected, and in some places petty persecution
and ill-feeling were slow to die.   Frequently the newspapers
ventured to suggest that there might be less acrimony in the
dispute.   As a result of the Disruption there was of course some
overlapping of agencies, particularly in the country ; and as
serious was the unhealthy type of religion encouraged, for
example, under " the Men " in the north of Scotland, and " a
cold and gloomy fanaticism " of which Norman Macleod
complains in the West Highlands.   The opinion of Thomas
Erskine of Linlathen is interesting :   " I doubt not that a
certain kind and degree of good may arise amongst certain
persons out of our Scotch Kirk Separation—more awakened
thought, more zeal—but I fear also more judging, more
spiritual pride, etc.—as in the much and perhaps overlauded
days of the Covenant."   " I have always expressed my conviction
that the movement was one more of a political than of a religious
character."   Sir William Hamilton the philosopher was also
unsympathetic, and published a pamphlet in which he sought
to prove that those who came out were " martyrs by mistake."
Those who stayed in were not guiltless of contributing to the
bitterness of the years of controversy.   The legal spirit in which
their side of the dispute was conducted, the hostile feeling which
began to invade the judicial mind under criticism and contra-
diction, the indignant tone of vested interests, the stiff adherence
of the Church to its rights of property in the case of *quoad sacra*
buildings, the refusal of sites for churches and the employment
of interdicts to prevent the use of premises, and cases of petty
persecution of employees, helped to foster general unbrotherliness.

II

The Christian good of the people of Scotland, however, was also furthered by those who remained with the Church of Scotland. This was due largely to the sheer fact of continuity and all that that implied. The excitement was on the other side ; but here there was a tradition that had absorbed and survived many a change, " the auld kirk," its very buildings, with a prestige and a sacredness that no others could acquire. The exciting makes itself noticeable, and its importance is apt to be overestimated. The other is not so evident but often just as real, and it has a strength of its own that is often underestimated. We seldom pay attention to what we are and have in common ; we notice much more the things in which we differ, our own special distinguishing features. It is the differences in ideas or even in looks that create much of the interest of human life ; but it is the ignored common element that is plainly fundamental. The Church of Scotland stood in a special sense for those things that are not affected by superficial change of conditions. The endurance and success of the Church are evidence of the solidity and worth of its contribution to the life of the people. The remarkable recovery after the devastating blow of the Disruption is witness that the Church meant something to the country for which there could be no substitute. During the Disruption dispute it had been relatively silent, and relatively silent it remained ; but " its silence was the token of depth and power." It stood for reserve rather than for anything like enthusiasm ; and for a community tone rather than for anything like an association of saints. Constitutionalism may also have its sacrifices, and there was much chivalry and loyalty and devotion and fortitude in the hearts of those that remained. " The root of all is order," said John Donne, poet and preacher, and this reminds us that the general type has not only persisted through Scottish history, but has played an important part in the history of other churches. " I am of the old opinion," said Tillotson, " that moderation is a virtue and one of the peculiar ornaments of our Church."

The Church of Scotland may also be said to have preserved

from loss at the period the cherished idea of the National Recognition of Religion, the doctrine that Christ is King of Nations as well as Head of the Church. A complete disruption of the Church from the State would have meant more than the loss of " temporalities." At the time of the Disruption too much emphasis was laid upon the financial aspect of the State connection, the " benefits of the Establishment," and too little on the national responsibilities of the Church. A sharpness of distinction was made between Church and State, between secular and sacred, that in no way corresponds to the facts of life. The world is not the evil thing that some have supposed, nor the State merely concerned with the life of the body. W. M. Hetherington could write : the Church's authority " cannot be derived from the State nor from anything worldly, since its very object is to oppose all worldliness " ; and further, " the province of the State is man's physical nature and condition, and its object to secure his well-being so far. . . . The province of the Church is man's moral and spiritual nature, and its object to rescue him from guilt and misery." But to-day there is a new sense of the unity of life and the intimate interrelation of activities and interests.

Further, there is a new sense of Community to which the Church must respond, and the idea of the national recognition of religion indicates its acknowledgment of its duty in this respect. We are concerned with more than privilege, financial, social and ceremonial, with more than the King's accession oath, his presence at Crathie Church, the formal visit of a Lord High Commissioner to our Assemblies, the appearance of the Assembly Moderator on platforms and at the microphone as the official representative of religion on special occasions, the invitation of the Moderator of Presbytery to public functions. These are all of value, perhaps of more value than the crude psychology of other days was aware. But there is more involved. These are days when the community is doing all sorts of things as community. People are working, thinking and amusing themselves much more together than they used to do ; we hear of the team spirit and of loyalty to the unit, and we know something of crowd psychology, and realize what has given appeal to totalitarianism in its various forms in political life. There is obviously some truth here represented, some need seeking satisfaction.

Certainly there is room for emphasis on the importance of the community for the individual. This has often been noted in connection with the community of the Church. Cyprian, Bucer and Calvin have insisted that it is only in and through the Church that the individual can be a Christian, and this is accepted by the whole Church when it thinks of itself as the body of Christ. Since the days of Aristotle it has been felt that only in the community is one a person at all. Isolation is death. Even Erastianism was ultimately an attempt to work religion into a suitable place in the communal scheme with some recognition of its communal significance. To-day, what we feel is rather that the community has a right to the Church's guidance on its communal problems, and has a right to communal religious expression. The Church has a duty to teach the community, and it will naturally expect to see the fruits of its teaching in public life and policy. The attitude of the country to all great problems concerns the Church. It wants the nation to be what it has so long professed to be, a Christian nation. These are days when the nation as such is in dealings with definitely non-Christian powers. The Church wishes our nation to take a Christian stand. France has been cited as a case of a country which has suffered in tone because of the abandonment of any direct connection between Church and State. The Church will not pretend to speak with authority on economic technicalities ; but it should be in a position to call attention fearlessly and persistently and with authority to the Christian spirit and the Christian standard, and to make it clear that it demands that measures taken whether with regard to home problems or international affairs must manifest that spirit and be compatible with that standard. Believing as we do in Christianity, it is our business to hold the country to its profession, and prevent the day when it might have no religious allegiance and the Church be banished once more to the Catacombs. It is important to maintain some direct connection between Church and State.

We must remember that the post-Disruption Church of
Scotland was neither a body of seventeenth-century Erastians
nor one of eighteenth-century Moderates such as appear in
Witherspoon's cartoon.   The last of that legion fell in the
campaign against the abolition of Patronage—dead as Queen
Anne and her Act.   It was of such that Lord Lorne was thinking
in the Disruption period when he said that the name
" Moderate " " has every recommendation but that of being
descriptive."   *The Wheat and the Chaff* shows that the
" residuary " Church of Scotland included along with 481
other ministers 260 who had professed Evangelical sympathies.
There was thus a healthy association of types from the beginning.
The Church as a whole, however, continued to favour a position
that was relatively Moderate, and has consistently employed its
double check on zeal through its combined conservatism and
latitudinarianism.   In this it represents the community check
upon the individual.   The Disruption Day was a glorious
triumph for the Evangelical party ; yet within a month it was
possible for Cunningham to remark : " In a certain sense we
have been beaten in this controversy."   The Church had not
been disrupted from the State.   Both the triumph and the
defeat have proved necessary to the position attained in 1929 ;
both Spiritual Independence and National Recognition of
Religion are enthroned in the Basis of Union.

III

The coming out and the staying in have alike had a share
in producing what is admittedly one of the best solutions yet
attempted of the age-long problem of the relation of Church
and State.   Lord Hugh Cecil, who was much interested in this
question, gave expression to unprejudiced outside opinion when
he declared that the Scottish arrangement " harmonises with
a definiteness and completeness for which I think no parallel
in Christian history is to be found the National Recognition of
Religion with the Spiritual Freedom of the Church."

Each party at the Disruption claimed to accept the doctrine
of Spiritual Independence, but they did not interpret the

expression in the same way. Historically the teaching may be traced to Calvin and the Scottish Reformers, who, of course, rested their faith on Scripture. An excellent statement of it was made by John Erskine of Dun in 1571, and it found a place in the *Westminster Confession*. In 1820 the General Assembly agreed that " the Independence of the Church of Scotland in all matters of faith, worship, and discipline, is fully established by law." But there was often trouble as to the content and limits of this conception of spiritual independence ; and Thomas Guthrie formed the impression that " the history of the Church of Scotland had been a history of aggression on the part of the State, of suffering and resistance on the part of the Church." The Disruption controversy involved the final conflict as to the proper relation of Church and State. The dominant party believed that it was acting within its rights in so applying the doctrine of spiritual independence as to pass the Veto Act and the Chapel Act. The decisions of the Law Courts gave what appeared to the Evangelicals an Erastian interpretation of the relations between the civil and the ecclesiastical authorities. The general background of the judgments seemed to be that there cannot be an *imperium in imperio*, or, as expressed by Lord Cottenham, " the idea of any power within the State not subject to the authority of the State is contrary to every principle of good government, and is not the law of Scotland." The Moderate party as a whole was not Erastian ; but it was certainly constitutionalist, and on the points in dispute felt the necessity of consultation and co-operation with the civil power.

After the Disruption the Church of Scotland accepted from the State measures which had at least the direction of both the Veto Act and the Chapel Act. The *Claim of Right*, after a detailed historical analysis, made the strongest assertion of the doctrine of the Headship of Christ, and demanded recognition of the inalienable liberties of a Church of Christ. But Sir Robert Peel, who refused this claim, had very plainly stated his mind that " to the Church belongs the exclusive jurisdiction in ecclesiastical matters. If, indeed, an attempt were made on the part of the civil courts to interfere with such

jurisdiction, there can scarcely be a question, I think, that
Parliament would step in, and confirm the authority of the
courts spiritual." The difficulty, therefore, was one of interpretation. No one was denying the spiritual independence of
the Church; but it required the Disruption to enable the
doctrine to be thoroughly examined, and the implications
realized and conflicting views adjusted. As now maintained,
the doctrine of Spiritual Independence is a constant reminder
that the Church refuses to be the organ of the secular power.
Religion has sometimes been simply a means by which a ruler
or governing class have held the people in control. Hobbes
thought it essentially an instrument of political and social
expediency; Marx regarded it as dope, and the recent history
of Germany and of the countries under Nazi sovereignty has
revealed conditions in which a claim to spiritual independence
is regarded as treasonable. The doctrine insists that the Church
stands above and outside of temporal circumstances and
represents the eternal point of view. The situation of a kingdom
within a kingdom arises when Law and Liberty are in direct
conflict, and might emerge were the community to cease to
accept the general Christian outlook. In such a case the
Church's duty to obey God rather than men would be clear and
persecution would be inevitable. There will always be limits
to what beliefs and practices society can tolerate; but it would
appear that under an enlightened democracy wide liberty is
possible, and the doctrine of the spiritual independence of the
Church reconcilable with the sovereignty of the law of the land.

In 1929 the Union of the Churches took place on the basis
of the United Free Church Act anent Spiritual Independence
(1906) and the Articles Declaratory of the Constitution of the
Church of Scotland in Matters Spiritual (1926). The relevant
section of the first reads as follows : " They assert and protest
that those branches of the Church of Christ in Scotland now
united in this Church have always claimed, and this Church
continues to claim, that the Church of Christ has under Him as
her only Head independent and exclusive jurisdiction and
power of legislating in all matters of doctrine, worship, discipline
and government of the Church, including therein the right

from time to time to alter, change, add to, or modify, her constitution and laws, Subordinate Standards, and Church Formulas, and to determine and declare what these are." Articles IV and V of the Church of Scotland read as follows :
" IV. This Church, as part of the Universal Church wherein the Lord Jesus Christ has appointed a government in the hands of Church office-bearers, receives from Him, its Divine King and Head, and from Him alone, the right and power subject to no civil authority to legislate, and to adjudicate finally, in all matters of doctrine, worship, government and discipline in the Church, including the right to determine all questions concerning membership and office in the Church, the constitution and membership of its Courts, and the mode of election of its office-bearers, and to define the boundaries of the spheres of labour of its ministers and other office-bearers. Recognition by civil authority of the separate and independent government and jurisdiction of this Church in matters spiritual, in whatever manner such recognition be expressed, does not in any way affect the character of this government and jurisdiction as derived from the Divine Head of the Church alone, or give to the civil authority any right of interference with the proceedings or judgments of the Church within the sphere of its spiritual government and jurisdiction.
" V. This Church has the inherent right, free from interference by civil authority, but under the safeguards for deliberate action and legislation provided by the Church itself, to frame or adopt its subordinate standards, to declare the sense in which it understands its Confession of Faith, to modify the forms of expression therein, or to formulate other doctrinal statements, and to define the relation thereto of its office-bearers and members, but always in agreement with the Word of God and the fundamental doctrines of the Christian Faith contained in the said Confession, of which agreement the Church shall be sole judge, and with due regard to liberty of opinion in points which do not enter into the substance of the Faith."
Very obviously State control in any Erastian sense is incompatible with these paragraphs. At the same time there is nothing in them at all incompatible with close relationship

between Church and State, and it only remained to formulate this helpfully. The National Recognition of Religion was accordingly put forward as a principle of the Church, and Articles III and VI of the Church of Scotland read as follows : " III. This Church is in historical continuity with the Church of Scotland which was reformed in 1560, whose liberties were ratified in 1592, and for whose security provision was made in the Treaty of Union of 1707. The continuity and identity of the Church of Scotland are not prejudiced by the adoption of these articles. As a national Church representative of the Christian Faith of the Scottish people it acknowledges its distinctive call and duty to bring the ordinances of religion to the people in every parish of Scotland through a territorial ministry.

" VI. This Church acknowledges the divine appointment and authority of the civil magistrate within his own sphere, and maintains its historic testimony to the duty of the nation acting in its corporate capacity to render homage to God, to acknowledge the Lord Jesus Christ to be King over the nations, to obey His laws, to reverence His ordinances, to honour His Church, and to promote in all appropriate ways the Kingdom of God. The Church and State owe mutual duties to each other, and acting within their respective spheres may signally promote each other's welfare. The Church and the State have the right to determine each for itself all questions concerning the extent and the continuance of their mutual relations in the discharge of these duties and the obligations arising therefrom."

The new position would have satisfied Dr Chalmers, who was so enthusiastic about the Establishment and about Spiritual Independence. It would have pleased John Knox, who earnestly sought State recognition and as earnestly declared that it was not essential. Eighteenth-century Moderates would have thought the terms Utopian, indeed might well have found them dangerous ; but only because our modern democratic conception of Liberty was in their day so far from being thinkable. Even in 1843 the Government was convinced that the degree of freedom which the Church was seeking they dared not dream of granting consistently with their duty to the security of the constitution. Government to-day has not the same problem to face. It is now established that very much fuller freedom of thought and action may be permitted to individuals and to groups, not only with entire safety to the community, but much to the advantage of the community, for that is strengthened by the people's interest and thought, by enterprise and experiment, by variety, by the development of personality—in a word, by Liberty.

Here, then, is the Church of Scotland one hundred years after the Disruption, united and comprehensive, strong through varied experience and a combination of proud traditions and crowning mercies, through the reconciliation of opposites with the loss of no principle that has proved of spiritual value ; free with a freedom that is enriched by the enabling relationship with the State ; democratic in the truest sense ; surely, by God's grace, as fit as can well be imagined for the task of a national Church in these days of challenge. This Church of Scotland, united, national, free and fit, is our Heritage from the past ; but Heritage spells responsibility, and our business now is to seek the Will of God for our time, and with all our heart and mind and strength make that Will be done. That the Church is so resolved is shown by its appointment in 1940 of a Commission for the Interpretation of God's Will in the present Crisis. This indicates that the future is to be faced, and faced with humble submission to the leading of God's good Spirit. It may well be faced with humility, for our Church, as it looks back, may do so with thankfulness, but not with self-satisfaction. In our story there has been much evidence of human weakness and sinfulness, and that we stand where we do to-day is of God's mercy. But the earnestness and thoroughness with which the Commission under the convenership of Professor John Baillie has been making its investigations, and the keen interest that has been manifested throughout the Church and far beyond in the results of its deliberations, are most promising features of the present situation and justify great expectations of a better future.

On 18th May 1843 Professor David Welsh preached the last sermon to the Church of Scotland before the Disruption.

His closing words may fitly conclude our commemorative study of that epoch-making event. " What the result of the present controversy may be cannot at present be known ; but we may rest assured, that in His own good time, the plans of Divine Providence will be fully disclosed ; and that all these things will work together for good to them that love the Lord, and are called according to His purpose. It furnishes matter of support and comfort, that valuable lessons are to be learned from the errors, as well as from the excellencies of the Church, as manifested in different periods ; so that by a right adjustment of well-selected parts from the temper and practices of the Church in past ages, there may be developed a harmonious whole. . . . These are the blessed times foretold in ancient prophecy, when Ephraim shall no longer vex Judah nor Judah Ephraim ; but when ' the Lord shall take the stick of Joseph which is in the hand of Ephraim, and the tribes of Israel his fellows, and shall put them with him, even with the stick of Judah, and make them one stick, and THEY SHALL BE ONE IN HIS HAND.' "

splendour of the dining-room. He had shown her a cold house, without love.

Now she looked at Paul, looked at his profile against the sky, the short blond ends of hair blowing in the wind. His strong hands were at ease on the wheel, and his feet planted on a familiar deck. Here was a man in his own element, a man she loved. And Charles had warned her not to lose him.

Suddenly she knew that it did not matter now that she owned the deck he stood on, that she owned the *Dolphin*, she owned the Pearl, and she owned Blake's Reach. She could not fully possess these things without the wisdom to use them in the right way, and the right way was not in fashioning them into a chain to bind Paul. He would always have more energy than discretion, more will to make money than skill in keeping it. But he had a dream, a vision, and his eyes were happily blinded by it. He wanted no fetters, and no burden of convention or tradition. She did not know if his dream of a kingdom to be won in the West Indies was something he would always keep, merely to carry before him as an eternal, unrealized hope, or whether he would attempt to turn it into a reality. Whatever he chose—to stay on the Marsh where he had been born, and to live out his life with her at Blake's Reach, or to seek the source of the dream in the West Indies— she would be with him. She had glimpsed the dream and the vision in Charles when he had elected to stay with Louise; it was this same shining thing she could never permit herself to destroy in Paul. If Blake's Reach had to be sacrificed to it, then it would be, and she would hold her peace.

And now she had to try to tell him this.

She called softly, "Paul. . . ."

He looked back at her, wearing the slight, familiar smile that warmed her.

EPILOGUE

IN THE grass-grown graveyard of St. Saviour's-by-the-Marsh are the headstones that mark the graves of Jane and Paul Fletcher; the tall grey slabs, weathering in the rains that sweep across the Marsh from the Channel, record no more than the bare facts of their names and ages. Beside them are the graves of those of their children who, being born on the Marsh, chose to live out their lives there. In the church itself a plain tablet, not a rose window, records the name of Charles Blake.

For Charles there is no marked grave. His headless body lies in quicklime, along with the others who perished during The Terror, in the cemetery of the Madeleine in Paris.

Nor is William's grave marked. He was lost when the *Raven*, largest vessel of the merchant fleet he had gathered together for trade between London and the West Indies, was wrecked off the island of Jamaica.